Rich,

To many more sales!

"Marc has presented many of the ideas in this book to our members and the feedback is always overwhelmingly positive! If you are looking to build your own high-velocity sales organization, then read every one of the concepts and tactics shared within these pages."

—Jeff Provost, Executive Director, EDPA

"You can see how Wayshak has worked on the front lines with leaders to develop sales programs. This book provides more implementable strategies than any other sales leadership book I've ever read. He has built on his other books and provided an executive blueprint. A must-read for every sales leader out there!"

—Michael Gavin, Senior Vice President, Cayan, LLC

"This is the definitive book for any sales leader looking to step on the gas and increase sales velocity! It's so much more than sales tactics. Marc forces you to think about who you have on your team, what they are doing, and how you track success. Awesome book!"

—Daniel Plante, Director of Sales and Marketing – North America & MCCA, John Bean Technologies Corporation

The

HIGH-VELOCITY

SALES

ORGANIZATION

THE SENIOR EXECUTIVE'S GUIDE TO ACCELERATING A SALES-DRIVEN COMPANY CULTURE

MARC WAYSHAK

This book is dedicated to my brilliant, insightful, and magnificent wife. You are the only reason that any of this exists.

Contents

The

HIGH-VELOCITY SALES ORGANIZATION

THE SENIOR EXECUTIVE'S GUIDE TO ACCELERATING A SALES-DRIVEN COMPANY CULTURE

high-velocity sales organization

noun

1. an organization with the right performers, strategy, and infrastructure in place, allowing it to dramatically increase sales by converting more opportunities at higher prices to more prospects.

Introduction

DOES YOUR BUSINESS world look different today than it did 10 years ago? How about 5 years ago? The truth is, of course, that the world of business is changing every day. In fact, the data shows that almost all industries are not just changing, but transforming. And the trend is only accelerating. This is particularly true for organizations that rely on sales teams to generate revenue. Yet, when was the last time you made a sustainable change to the way your organization sells?

Talent is increasingly difficult to find, traditional selling no longer works, and salespeople are more distracted than ever before.

I decided to write this book after years of watching senior executives try to address today's sales issues with yesterday's strategies. These smart, highly qualified men and women put their organizations in peril simply because they haven't adjusted to the new reality: Talent is increasingly difficult to find, traditional selling no longer works, and salespeople are more distracted than ever before.

These leaders often react to unexpected changes by doubling down on their existing tactics. They make decisions based on gut instinct. They lead with intuition over strategy. In doing so, these leaders cause a lot of their own problems, failing to react quickly to new situations. Their organizations are destined for trouble.

But a select few leaders understand that they must embrace change, recognize past mistakes, and move quickly to adapt. These senior executives react to unwanted news and unexpected changes with a willingness to learn and change with the times. Their teams have potential for greatness. A high-velocity sales organization is what will get them there. The mere fact that you've picked up this book means you're likely to be one of these leaders who's willing to adapt to our changing world.

Leading a high-velocity sales organization requires having the right performers, strategy, and infrastructure in place, allowing your organization to dramatically increase sales by converting more opportunities at higher prices to more prospects.

You might think that this "high-velocity sales thing" is the difference between being good and being great—to take a page from Jim Collins. But I would argue that it's actually far more profound. It's really the difference between massive success and utter failure. In today's business world, where changes are happening so fast, so frequently, this new approach to sales isn't merely suggestive for your organization. It's required.

Leading a high-velocity sales organization requires having the right performers, strategy, and infrastructure in place.

In fact, the fast-increasing rate of dynamic change is affecting businesses of all sizes in unprecedented ways. Since 2000 alone, a whopping 52% of Fortune 500 companies have either gone bankrupt, been acquired, or disappeared completely.[1] At the current rate, about 50% of all S&P 500 firms will be replaced by 2027.[2]

Even the most successful companies are going bankrupt. While the average life expectancy of a Fortune 500 firm was around 75 years in 1960, today it's less than 15 years—and declining all the time.[3]

Specifically in the world of sales, the data is equally bleak. The average tenure of a VP of sales has dropped precipitously, from 26 months in 2010 to 19 months in 2017.[4] Across all industries and geographies, quota attainment has dropped, too, from 63% of salespeople in 2012 to 53% in 2016.[5]

Since 2000 alone, a whopping 52% of Fortune 500 companies have either gone bankrupt, been acquired, or disappeared completely.

What are the drivers behind this undeniable downward turn in sales?

The first cause of this alarming trend is one I'm willing to bet you've experienced firsthand: Talent is increasingly hard to find. The dearth of available sales talent is so extreme, many organizations have already given up when it comes to hiring promising new talent. Research shows that up to 40% of companies are struggling to find the talent they need.[6]

In 2017, the unemployment rate for sales professionals dropped from 4.6% to 3.8%.[7] When you factor out the chronically unemployed, that means unemployment for the talented folks you want to hire is essentially zero. Finding the right people for your sales team is infinitely more challenging today than it has been in former economic times.

We're looking at a war for talent: 45% of HR managers currently have jobs they can't fill because they can't find qualified talent, and 58% report that they have jobs that stay open for 12 weeks or longer.[8]

The second massive change in sales is that traditional selling strategies—the ones we've all depended on for so long—just don't work anymore. We know this because only 18% of salespeople today are classified by buyers as trusted advisors whom they respect.[9]

The top reason why these old-school selling techniques don't work anymore is that prospects have more access to information than ever before. While the traditional selling paradigm is based entirely around the idea that buyers need salespeople to give them information, this is increasingly less true. In fact, 57% of salespeople say that buyers today are less dependent on them during the buying process than they were just a few years ago.[10] And in a recent survey I conducted, 61.4% of salespeople said that it's harder or much harder to sell today than it was five years ago.[11]

61% of consumers and 76% of business buyers say they feel significantly more empowered than they did just five years ago.

What's more, the average buyer today has no patience or need for a sales pitch. Over 80% of buyers don't even want to connect with a salesperson during the initial awareness stage of their buying process.[12]

And why would they? The average mobile phone today is millions of times more powerful than all of NASA's combined computing power in 1969,[13] so buyers literally have the world at their fingertips. It's no wonder that 61% of consumers and 76% of business buyers say they feel significantly more empowered than they did just five years ago.[14] The world is shrinking. Not only can prospects get whatever information they want, whenever they want it, but they can get it from anywhere in the world.

Just a few years ago, your biggest competitors may have been down the street from you, or a few cities over. But today, nearly every industry is dealing with massive degrees of international competition.

By 2020, there will be at least four Internet-connected devices for every person on Earth.[15] With the implementation of algorithms and artificial intelligence (AI), technology is starting to dramatically replace the day-to-day salespeople we always considered critical to the front lines of sales. (In reality, one million sales reps will be out of a job by 2020.)[16]

Companies like NorthFace are already using IBM's Watson AI platform to customize highly detailed client orders,[17] while thousands of everyday companies use chat-bots to communicate live with clients.

68% of salespeople are behaving in ways that actually drive down performance in sales.

By ignoring this clear-cut shift in the way information is exchanged with prospects today, a staggering 68% of salespeople are behaving in ways that actually drive down performance in sales.[18] This will only continue as access to information gets easier, faster, and more ubiquitous.

This brings us to the third and final factor that's transforming sales as we know it. Salespeople are more distracted and aimless than they've ever been. On average, sales reps today only spend 36% of their time selling.[19] What are they doing the other 64% of the time? It's an important question that most companies can't answer.

Part of this problem is due to a virtual overload of technology tools in sales. More organizations are doubling down to introduce tech that helps salespeople manage their time and be more efficient. Ironically, these efforts frequently make salespeople less efficient with their time. In fact, 55% of all sales reps believe their company's sales tools actually hinder their performance, while 59% feel like they have to use too many sales tools.[20]

Far too often, salespeople get stuck on the front lines, endlessly entering data into systems that no one ever looks at. And while some companies are becoming highly empowered by technological changes—adapting quickly and implementing the best new tools—others are becoming crippled by the introduction of even the simplest CRMs.

Management infrastructure is often weak simply because companies are trying to keep up with technology, rather than use it to their advantage. That's why infrastructure is a sharp divider for companies today. At its core, strong infrastructure is the right combination of sales leadership, CRM practices, and accountability processes needed to drive day-to-day sales activity—and combat the pervasive distraction that's crushing sales productivity.

55% of all sales reps believe their company's sales tools actually hinder their performance.

When this infrastructure is missing, sales organizations get bogged down by the very tools and systems that are supposed to help them thrive.

The key to overcoming these major hurdles in sales today is to create a high-velocity sales organization.

High-velocity sales organizations overcome these challenges by implementing a three-part framework that gives them the right performers, the right strategy, and the right infrastructure. This is accomplished by achieving a consistent flow of top performers, a self-improving and highly adaptive sales strategy, and a clear system for building out the right sales infrastructure with the right technology.

In my work with hundreds of companies helping senior executives create high-velocity sales organizations, I've had a bird's-eye view of what is and isn't working to combat today's top sales challenges. Combine that with a data-driven, science-based approach to sales, and I've developed a system for dramatically increasing sales by implementing the fewest possible changes at your organization.

The purpose of this book is to show you exactly how. By implementing my three-part framework for performers, strategy, and infrastructure, you'll have the tools to adapt to any major sales challenge that comes across your organization's purview.

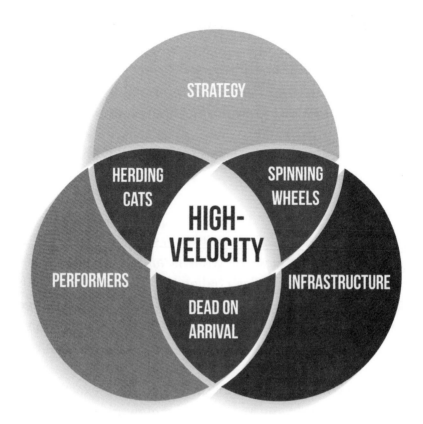

As this visual shows, you really need all three components to be a high-velocity sales organization. The lack of any of these three elements will lead to problems in overcoming key sales challenges today.

For example, if you have strategy and infrastructure in place, but you lack performers, then you'll just be spinning your wheels. If you have performers and infrastructure, but not the right strategy, then your salespeople are dead on arrival: They won't be able to sell because they'll be perceived as low-value in the eyes of prospects. And finally, if you have performers and strategy, but you lack infrastructure, you'll be herding cats. There will be no way to ensure your salespeople are doing the right things on a day-to-day basis.

It's important to note that you don't have to move every dial I mention in this book. You simply need to determine the most important dials for your organization today—and start to tweak those dials in smart ways. This isn't about making sweeping changes. It's about identifying those specific areas where you'll get the highest return for your effort to improve.

And one more thing: These changes must be implemented from the top of your organization, because sales culture is driven from the top. It doesn't come from sales managers, but rather from the CEO, the president, or the CSO. While your managers can implement the strategy you come up with, the decision to make those changes must come from *you*, the senior executive. Ultimately, having that senior-level discipline around these changes will be the difference between dramatic, powerful results at your organization—or just another fad that the boss introduced.

Marc Wayshak

Section I

Performers

AT THE DAWN of the thirteenth century, Genghis Kahn was on the cusp of changing the course of history. Today, we know him as the fierce Mongolian warrior who conquered more than twice as much land as any other ruler to date. But in 1206, while the 44-year-old Khan had already unified the sprawling nomadic tribes of Northeast Asia, he hadn't yet reached beyond the steppes of Central Asia.

Seeking to expand his empire, Khan sent ruthless invasions out in virtually every direction. By the time of his death in 1227, just 21 years later, the Mongolian Empire stretched from the Pacific Ocean to the Caspian Sea.

How did just one man so radically transform the destiny of the Mongols in such a short span of time? The answer, of course, is that just one man didn't.

No matter how large an army Khan commanded, he still couldn't have led the Mongols on such a spectacular trajectory all on his own. Luckily, he didn't have to try: Khan surrounded himself with ranks of highly competent, qualified military leaders who shared his vision and his acumen for war. He balked at appointing his family members to military posts based on blood ties alone. This was a stark break from tradition at the time. Instead, Khan sought talented fighters and strategic thinkers who could be trusted to do the job—regardless of social rank or family lineage.

Khan was so committed to recruiting talented military men that he even hired his fiercest enemies for the job. In 1201, while fighting to unify the Mongol tribes, Khan was struck in the neck with an arrow. The arrow was shot by a man named Jebe, who had managed to maneuver past the great Khan elite guard to strike the blow. Khan survived the attack, and his army won the battle.

What became of Jebe? Khan not only let his would-be assassin live; he also appointed him as a top general to lead part of his army.

Genghis Kahn understood the power of top performers. He was willing to put ego aside when it came to building the strongest organization of warriors he possibly could. If a man was skilled enough to nearly kill him, then surely he was skilled enough to help lead Khan's soldiers to victory. No matter where it came from, talent was never wasted around Genghis Khan. Instead, it was swiftly incorporated into the well-oiled machine of top performers that made his empire flourish.

As you begin to build your own high-velocity sales organization, it's imperative that you, too, understand the immense power of top performers.

I know it can seem that every moving part of your organization is equally important. You need the right sales process, or else you're missing out on tremendous opportunities to close more sales. You need the most effective infrastructure for your sales team, or else there's no accountability. And what's more, you need top sales performers working at your company, or else you're just spinning your wheels.

But there's a reason why I'm starting this book with a focus on the performers at your organization, and the story of Genghis Khan explains it. Your top performers are the determined workers, ambitious warriors, and strategic thinkers who

> *The annual turnover rate in sales is twice the national average.*

will enable your sales army to thrive above the competition.

If you can only focus on one moving part to start building your high-velocity sales organization right now, this is it.

While 1 out of every 9 employees in the U.S. works in sales—making it the second-largest occupation in the country[21]—the annual turnover rate in sales is twice the national average.[22] What's more, over half of all current salespeople would be better-suited to an alternative career—and a quarter of capable salespeople are hired to fill the wrong sales positions.[23] There's never been a more pressing time to get clear on who your top performers are, how to hire them, and how to keep them at your organization.

Chapter 1:

The Power of Performers

SIMPLY PUT, IDENTIFYING, recruiting, and retaining top performers is the single most important part of your job as a company leader. You can have the right strategy and infrastructure in place, but if you don't have the right people, you're still headed for disaster. Even if you have zero strategy and infrastructure in place, as long as you have the right people on board, you'll ultimately be in a better place. (Although, I wouldn't just stop there.)

I can't stress this enough: If you skip over everything I'm about to tell you about performers, the rest of this book will be meaningless. Learning how to identify, recruit, and retain top sales performers is by far the most meaningful change you can make to improve your company.

You still might not be convinced that this is part of your job description as CEO, COO, CSO, or even as director of sales. If that's the case, I want you to switch gears from sales to sports for just a minute.

Consider Bill Belichick, who had led the Patriots to eight Super Bowl appearances at the time of writing this book. Widely considered one of the best coaches in the NFL,

Belichick has a core competency that's somewhat surprising: identifying talent that others don't see.

Belichick is famous for rooting out unknown, unrecognized players who have potential for greatness on the field, but haven't yet demonstrated it fully. He then brings these performers onto his team, where they become part of the world-class infrastructure and strategy he's put in place. But everything starts with this idea of identifying talent.

You're the head coach of your company or division. It's your job to do exactly what Belichick does, or else you're no different from a world-class football coach with a team full of bad athletes. Everything starts here.

WHAT IS A TOP PERFORMER?

All this begs the question, what exactly *is* a top performer—and how can you tell when you've got an A player on your hands?

When I first sit down with my consulting clients, I ask them to make a list of every salesperson in the company and score them on a typical A to F scale. I show them the chart below to create a basis for rating performers, and to avoid rating performers based on pure gut instinct. Once we have all the salespeople listed and scored, it becomes exponentially easier to figure out who the best and worst performers are—and why.

Here's the graph I share with my clients to help them score the sales team. It lists the key attributes shared by most A, B, C, D, and F players:

	A and A- Players	B+, B, B- Players	C+, C, C- Players	D and F Players
Approach	Consultative	More transactional	Totally transactional	Failing
Sale Size	Huge	Mid-size	Small and mid-size	Failing
Prospecting	Consistent and strategic	Somewhat consistent and often less strategic	Inconsistent, without strategy	Failing
Prospect Profile	C-level	Managers	Buyers	Failing
Coachability	Highly coachable	Moderately coachable	Difficult to coach	Failing
Quota Attainment	Consistently exceeds quota	Consistently hits quota	Consistently misses quota	Failing

We'll come back to this chart in the next chapter when we rate your existing sales team.

ALL MUST BE ≤ B-

The first point to remember about this method of rating salespeople is that anyone you rate as *below* a B- has got to be replaced. That's your entire C, D, and F player list. Don't even waste time including these salespeople in the rest of the discussion. Why? Because they're actively hurting your sales efforts in two key ways.

First, B- and below players are the types of people who take up a lot of managers' time. They need help with pretty much everything, from prospecting effectively to hitting the easiest sales goals. Second, they're not even making an ROI for the company—and they never will.

Now, I'm not suggesting you just outright fire all the salespeople you rate as below a B-. What I'm suggesting is that you remove them *immediately* from sales and your sales growth efforts. You can transfer them to another department in your organization if they have potential for a different job. But they don't belong in sales.

Don't feel guilty about this. Chances are, these salespeople are going home each day to complain to their significant other about how much they hate their job; how challenging it is; how they can never seem to catch a break. (They're also probably complaining to others on your sales team, tainting the well.) These folks fall into the category of the 61% of salespeople who never intended to go into sales in the first place.[24] They also cost big money: A single bad sales hire can cost your organization as much as $616,000.[25] If they're simply not a good fit for the sales role, it's your job to get them out.

> *A single bad sales hire can cost your organization as much as $616,000.*

That said, it's important not to write off a salesperson for the wrong reasons. Just because someone is a B- right now doesn't mean they don't have the potential to be a B or B+ player in the near future. Use your intuition to make the call. That B- salesperson with great potential is a very different story from one who's a C player today and could only be a C+ at best in the future. That person has absolutely got to go.

A ≥ 2B

B players themselves aren't bad performers; they're just not nearly as exceptional as A players. B players are solid performers who tend to be relatively consistent producers. But they also have a tendency to miss opportunities you would have closed yourself. They're more transactional than consultative, and they hit more singles than doubles—and almost never home runs.

A players, on the other hand, are constantly hitting home runs. That's why every A player is worth at least two B players from a revenue perspective. A players close many multiples more than B players do, and they consistently sell to high-level prospects in the executive suite. Consider that only 31% of salespeople are able to effectively converse with senior executives, and you start to understand how valuable A players are.[26]

Only 31% of salespeople are able to effectively converse with senior executives.

In fact, one A player typically carries the weight of at least two B players on the team. This is more representative of just how good A players are, rather than a knock on the talent of B players. A players don't just build relationships with clients; they create value with and for them.

This isn't just my opinion. Gong.io, one of the world's leading conversion intelligence platforms for sales, has groundbreaking data that supports this idea. They've analyzed nearly a million sales conversations to determine what separates A players from average performers in sales.

What they found is striking: When speaking with prospects, top-performing salespeople ask nearly double the number of business-related questions per hour than average performers do. They also listen to prospects a whole lot more—approximately 50% more.[27] This data shows that A players really do perform behaviors that consistently build better relationships with clients and create more value for the sale.

CASE STUDY: A PLAYERS

Here's a real-life example that demonstrates the power of A players over B players. One of my former client companies, with $25 million in annual revenues, had eight total salespeople. Out of the eight salespeople, there was one sales guy, Jared, who pulled in $12 million on his own. That's one salesperson carrying the weight of seven other people.

This might sound like an extreme example, but it's actually not that uncommon. It's a testament to the power of identifying those A players who are a true gift to your organization. They can make you incredible amounts of money, but they don't come along often. You can poach them from other companies, but you're more likely to hire someone who starts off as a B or B+ player, and later develops into an A player.

Unfortunately, it can be difficult to retain A players, mainly because they're so valuable. They tend to run off and start their own businesses or become CEOs. (If you're reading this book right now, I'm willing to bet you might have been an A player salesperson at some point in your past.) A players think big, they always want to grow, and they're incredibly talented at what they do.

Jared was only willing to stick around in sales because he was making so much money—$500,000 a year, plus equity—that he outearned the CEO. Keep this in mind as we continue. We'll take a closer look at how to retain top sales talent in Chapter 3.

Next, I'm going to walk you through the most effective way to analyze your existing sales team. I'll give you a clear lens through which you can view your team in an unbiased way.

Later on, I'm also going to show you exactly what traits to look for in new talent, and how to assess those measurable traits during the hiring process. For now, let's focus on evaluating your existing team so you can identify what you're currently working with.

Chapter 2:

Take a Look in the Mirror

NOW THAT WE'VE covered the basics of how to rate salespeople on an A to F scale, it's time to do a quick, powerful exercise to analyze your existing sales team. There's one fundamental question you want to be able to answer by the end of this chapter: *What are you working with right now?*

Here are the three key takeaways you'll get from this exercise:

1. Identify the real top performers on your team: B players and above with a positive ROI who are making your organization money

2. Pinpoint which salespeople have the most potential to become A players, and resolve to invest in them and help them grow

3. Determine which salespeople simply aren't a good fit for sales, and develop a plan to move them quickly off the sales team

Before we begin, let me just say this: The number one mistake I see companies make is that they hold on to their under-performing salespeople for far too long. A fifth of employers who make a bad hire say they knew within the first week that they'd made a mistake—and more than half knew within three weeks.[28] Still, they kick the can down the road, thinking maybe those C players will come around and start hitting their goals eventually.

78% of high-performing sales organizations say they would terminate underperformers within a year.

They never do.

Studies show that the highest-performing sales organizations are also the quickest to terminate under-performers. While 78% of high-performing sales organizations say they would terminate under-performers within a year, only 63% of average and 52% of under-performing sales organizations say the same.[29] If you've been thinking about whether to terminate under-performers on your own team, let this exercise be the catalyst to help you finally make the call.

Now we're ready to start.

Step 1: Remember this chart from Chapter 1? Refer back to these key points about A, B, C, D, and F players to help you fill out the Current and Potential Letter Scores for each salesperson on your team:

	A and A- Players	B+, B, B- Players	C+, C, C- Players	D and F Players
Approach	Consultative	More transactional	Totally transactional	Failing
Sale Size	Huge	Mid-size	Small and mid-size	Failing
Prospecting	Consistent and strategic	Somewhat consistent and often less strategic	Inconsistent, without strategy	Failing
Prospect Profile	C-level	Managers	Buyers	Failing
Coachability	Highly coachable	Moderately coachable	Difficult to coach	Failing
Quota Attainment	Consistently exceeds quota	Consistently hits quota	Consistently misses quota	Failing

Step 2: Take out a sheet of paper and draw out the following scorecard, creating enough rows for every salesperson on your team. (Don't fill this out in the book—you want to make sure your ratings are kept confidential and won't be accidentally shared with others who might be sensitive to the contents.)

In addition to scoring every salesperson on your team, I want you to write down One Sentence Why for each score. For this part, simply jot down your reasoning behind each salesperson's score—both current and potential.

Name	Current Letter Score	One Sentence Why This Is the Current Score	Potential Letter Score	One Sentence Why This Is the Potential Score

 You can download a free PDF version of this chart in my Key Pages & Worksheets Guide at www.MarcWayshak.com/HighVelocity.

Step 3: Review your chart. Are there any surprises? Take some time to read through everything you wrote. It's really powerful to see your thoughts on the entire sales team all in one place.

Step 4: Highlight or underline the names of salespeople who have the highest Potential Letter Score. Ask yourself the following questions about each salesperson in this category:

- What can you do this week to start developing the full potential of this salesperson? (We will explore this more later on in this book.)

- What are the areas that this salesperson needs the most help with—and how can you facilitate help in those areas?

- What's holding this salesperson back from being at that Potential Letter Score right now?

Step 5: Next, highlight or underline the names of salespeople who scored below a B- for Potential Scores. Ask yourself the following question about each salesperson in this category:

- If this salesperson were to leave the sales team tomorrow, would you need someone else to take his or her spot?

- Is this salesperson in charge of a specific territory or list you'd need someone else to manage?

- Based on your current sales structure, would you need to eventually replace this salesperson with a new hire?

- Or, could you just reshuffle the decks of your existing team and get by with fewer people once this salesperson is gone?

CASE STUDY: REPLACE OR RESHUFFLE

The answer to whether you should replace a salesperson or simply reshuffle the decks will vary widely from organization to organization. For example, one client of mine has eight salespeople, and each salesperson manages a specific region of the country where they meet face-to-face with clients on a regular basis. Because of this, it's critical for that company to have eight salespeople in place. If they let two salespeople go, they must replace them with two more—and fast.

On the flip side, another client of mine has a team of 75 salespeople. They recently went through this process of evaluating and scoring their existing team, and ultimately decided that eight salespeople had to go. Since these salespeople weren't stuck in specific geographies, the company could let them go without replacing them. Instead, they just reshuffled the decks, moving around the remaining salespeople to take on more accounts.

In the end, this company was able to increase sales. With 75 salespeople, revenues had been $145 million; after losing eight salespeople, revenues increased to $159 million with a smaller team of 67 sales reps.

How is that possible? By making a few tweaks to the sales strategy and infrastructure—which we'll discuss later on in this book—and reallocating key accounts to the top performers on the team, the entire sales organization simply worked better. In a word, it became high-velocity.

Now that you've taken the time to carefully evaluate your current sales team, you should have a clear view of what you're working with. You now have a concise list that shows who your top performers are, and why; who your bottom performers are, and how you plan to deal with them; and who has the most potential for high performance, and how to develop their talent (more to come on that later).

The next question is, *Are you going to need to fill an open spot on your sales team soon?* Or, can you take your time and let the hiring process run its course? In either case, what should that process look like? Luckily, we're about to dive deep into recruiting and hiring—two of the most important areas for any company out there.

Chapter 3:

Attracting Top Talent

BEFORE YOU START recruiting, you need to understand what you're looking for. That means establishing a clear Ideal Candidate Profile. This is a specific outline of the type of salesperson who would fit in well at your organization, and ultimately generate huge revenues for your company.

It's the most important place to start because, without a clear profile, you can't have an effective recruiting strategy. And that only means one thing: mis-hires.

At companies around the globe, the mis-hire rate clocks in at an astounding 80%.[30] This is no small problem, and your Ideal Candidate Profile is the first step to addressing it.

Now it's time to create your own profile. The key to this exercise is to paint a picture, with broad strokes, of what you want in a salesperson. In the next section, we'll tighten this up based on actual, measurable traits you want to look for in talent. But right now, let's focus on outlining that ideal candidate for your top sales positions.

Fill out the scorecard on the following page, focusing on your Must-haves and your Wants. This is pretty straightforward.

Must-haves are non-negotiable. Maybe your ideal salesperson absolutely must have mastery of a certain hard skill, willingness to travel 40% of the time, or a competitive attitude. Perhaps geography is set in stone, too, and the salesperson needs to be in Boston or Chicago—nowhere else. These would be Must-haves.

Your Wants could be industry experience, experience with Salesforce CRM, or experience selling to C-suite prospects. Whatever it is that you'd consider to be a plus, but not crucial to success on your sales team.

It's your turn:

Ideal Candidate Scorecard

	Must-haves	Wants
Skills		
Experience		
Personality Traits		
Salary (Comp vs. Base)		
Geography (Travel? Remote? In-Office?)		
Other		

 You can download a free PDF version of this chart in my Key Pages & Worksheets Guide at www.MarcWayshak.com/HighVelocity.

CASE STUDY: THE PITFALLS OF NO PROFILE

To underscore the importance of taking your Ideal Candidate Profile seriously, I'd like to tell you about one of my former clients, Susan. Susan is the CEO of a marketing company who had hired several salespeople through networking. When she brought me in to help her struggling sales team, I asked her a simple question: "What traits did those salespeople all share in common that caused you to hire them?"

Susan had no answer.

In fact, we could find very few characteristics in common among her last five hires. As a result, her sales team was all over the place. Some required a ton of training and had little experience in sales. Others were veteran salespeople who were stuck with bad habits, unable to hit their goals. None of them shared much in common by way of approach, personality, or sales strategy.

The fact is that Susan could have avoided this whole headache had she taken the time to create an Ideal Candidate Profile. But without one, she was shooting in the dark, hiring whoever came along.

AVOID "EXTRANEOUS TRAITS"

Now that you have your Ideal Candidate Profile laid out, take a moment to ask yourself: "Am I focusing on traits that *really matter*?" Many executives get distracted by what I call "extraneous traits" that they perceive to be valuable in salespeople—but in reality, those traits have little or nothing to do with sales success.

Take my client Gary, for example. Gary is the CEO of a $150 million services company. When Gary and I first started working together to hire new salespeople for his team, he only cared about one thing: athletes. As long as a candidate had a background in sports, Gary was sold. He even listed "former or current athlete" as a Must-have in his Ideal Candidate Profile. Gary assumed all athletes were naturally competitive, had a strong work ethic, and were born top performers. And while that certainly *can* be true, it isn't always.

As someone who was an All-American college athlete, I can tell you that a lot of people who play sports should never be in sales. In fact, many of my former rugby and football teammates would crumble in a selling role. While they might have been great at passing or tackling, many lacked far more desirable traits—like consistency, sense of drive, or strategic thinking.

> *The myth of the extroverted, highly social sales performer is pervasive.*

So, if someone was an athlete once upon a time, it shouldn't have mattered to Gary. Someone who did drama in high school or college might be a far better salesperson than the captain of the high school football team. It's purely heuristics to say that athletes will be good at sales. Avoid this pitfall—and others like it—at all costs.

Let's take a look at another extraneous trait to avoid, perhaps the most common in sales hiring: extroversion. The myth of the extroverted, highly social sales performer is pervasive. Ask nearly anyone to describe a top salesperson, and the word "extroverted" is sure to come up.

But the data has something different to say about this widespread sales ideal.

In a recent study, introverted salespeople were found to generate slightly less money per hour than extroverts, but here's the twist: The higher the salespeople scored for extroversion, the lower their performance fell. The highest performers were actually neither introverts nor extroverts, but rather ambiverts, whose personality traits fall exactly in between. In the study, these ambiverts blew their counterparts out of the water, earning nearly 60% more than both introverts and extroverts did.[31]

MAKE SURE IT'S LEGAL!

I hope it goes without saying, but you can't discriminate when you hire—even if you think you're putting a positive spin on it. Your Must-haves and Wants absolutely cannot include traits such as the candidate's age, gender, or physical appearance.

My client Bill is the perfect example of how executives unwittingly create illegal criteria for hiring. When I first asked Bill who his ideal salespeople were, he immediately responded, "I want young people who are real go-getters!" Not only is it illegal to hire someone based on age, but this is also similar to the athletes heuristic we discussed before. Not all young people are go-getters, as we all know. A candidate's age doesn't have any bearing on their level of motivation in the workplace.

Bill also told me that he wanted to hire a team of attractive salespeople. Wrong, again! While we don't want people who look unprofessional or dress poorly, it's a dangerous game of semantics to put this in your hiring criteria. Expect professionalism, but know that there is very little correlation between looks and success in sales. Having worked personally with hundreds of A player salespeople over the years, I can tell you that they come in all different physical packages.

WHO'S IN CHARGE?

One of the most common questions I hear from executives is, "Where can I find more talent?" It's often the first thing they ask in an initial meeting. This isn't surprising, as finding quality sales talent is one of the biggest challenges executives face. The data shows that recruiting and retaining sales talent isn't just difficult—it's also costly. The annual turnover rate for inside and outside sales roles is an average of 26%, with an average cost per turnover of $97,690.[32]

The truth is, there's no magic bullet to solve this problem. It's similar to when a struggling salesperson asks, "Where can I find more leads?" The answer is never simple. Salespeople have to roll up their sleeves and do the grunt work to find more clients. It might not happen right away, but a strategic, consistent prospecting approach will ultimately yield more clients for any salesperson.

As it turns out, attracting top talent to your organization isn't much different.

I said this in Chapter 1, but it bears repeating: Identifying, recruiting, and retaining top talent is the single most important thing you can do as a leader in your organization. In particular, recruiting top-line revenue generators to join your company is essential.

Even Fortune 500 CEOs are out there in the field, looking for the next A player who single-handedly earns more for the company than multiple other salespeople combined—sometimes up to 10 of them. (Yes, I've really seen it.)

Attracting top sales talent like this to your organization should be at least 25% of your job as CEO, president, VP of sales, COO, or any senior leadership role. Unsurprisingly, sales positions are the highest priority roles to fill at companies today, according to a recent LinkedIn survey on global recruiting trends.[33]

Only you have the authority to make tough decisions about recruiting and hiring.

So why do so many executives pass off this increasingly critical task to low-level employees?

A study by the *Harvard Business Review* found that merely 50% of those recruited for positions within the top three tiers of the company—that is, C-level executives, their direct reports, and those right below them—were ever interviewed by anyone in the C-suite.[34] This is consistent with what goes on at most sales organizations, where the majority of senior executives delegate the recruitment of top sales talent to someone whose earnings don't depend on the top-line or bottom-line success of the company.

It just doesn't make sense to let employees like this handle a task as highly strategic—and critically important to top and bottom-line revenues—as the recruitment of top sales talent. They simply cannot take full ownership of your recruitment or hiring process. It's your job to lay out the strategy—not theirs. It's your job to think strategically—not theirs. Only you have the authority to make tough decisions about recruiting and hiring.

If you're still not convinced, just look at the numbers. Hiring a superstar salesperson could mean millions more in revenues each year for your company. Conversely, hiring a single wrong salesperson could cost you big—up to $616,000.[35] Yet we often choose to put this entire process into the hands of someone who doesn't have bottom-line responsibilities.

Does that sound reasonable to you? Of course not.

DIY RECRUITING IS A MUST

That's all well and good, but most executives still balk at the idea of taking ownership of recruiting sales talent. For one thing, they just don't know where to start.

First off, it's important to note that I'm not suggesting you alone should do 100% of the recruiting for your sales team. That would be an impossible task for any senior leader. But as I said earlier in this chapter, recruiting top talent should be at least 25% of your job. And that means DIY recruiting is a must.

What is DIY recruiting? It's an ongoing method of approaching your job with an eye out for top talent. It's about constantly putting out nets and laying out feelers for superstar salespeople. It's about developing relationships with top performers in the industry—way before they ever express interest in working for your company. And it's about doing *some of your own recruiting* for the absolute best people in your industry.

The top three sources for quality hires for most organizations are social professional networks such as LinkedIn (40%), third-party websites or online job boards (46%), and employee referrals (48%).[36] We'll discuss all three in this section.

I know this sounds daunting, especially if you've previously delegated recruiting to your HR team. So I've put together this step-by-step guide to jump-start your own DIY recruiting process:

1. Implement a generous sales hire referral reward program.

This is one of the easiest steps to DIY recruiting, but it also gives you the most leverage. Offer a generous referral reward to anyone who can find you a candidate to hire in sales. Don't cut costs here. Think of what an outside recruiter would charge to find top sales talent (we'll talk more about that later). Your referral reward should be at least $5K. Go big here.

Companies tend to be stingy with referral rewards, but that's a big mistake. Implement an aggressive sales hire referral reward program at your organization instead. No one is inspired by a $500 reward. But $5K? That's a different story. Make your rewards contingent upon the new hire sticking around for at least three months. And don't just focus on your employees for referrals—some of your top referrals will come from your client base and your vendors. Your clients and vendors see your competitors out there every day, and they can be one of the best sources of potential referrals, so include them in your program, too.

2. Leverage your employees' LinkedIn connections.

Organize quarterly meetings with your sales team to go through their LinkedIn connections. This is a powerful way to find superstar salespeople who are already in your organization's network. Don't just ask your salespeople, "Who do you know that might be a good fit on our sales team?" Instead, actually sit down with each salesperson and go through their LinkedIn connections.

You can filter through your employees' connections by sorting for those who work in sales. Then have your employees walk you through any strong profiles that come up. Let your bonus incentive fire your employees up to reach out to potential candidates.

Employee referrals are the number one channel for quality hires, bringing in 48% of top talent to organizations.

This process works wonders to drum up names for potential candidates. It's no surprise that employee referrals are the number one channel for quality hires, bringing in 48% of top talent to organizations, according to a recent LinkedIn study.[37] Your own salespeople are your absolute best option.

3. Network at industry gatherings.

Networking at events is one of the most effective ways to find top sales talent—but it won't happen overnight. You have to constantly show up to industry gatherings, connect with your peers, and listen closely for talk about top performers. Find out who's winning the sales awards in your industry and keep tabs on who's the talk of the town.

You don't have to directly recruit anyone at these events; you just want to keep your ear to the ground. Stay in the know and eventually you'll be on the radar of top performers, too.

To take action on this step, write out a list of events over the next 12 months where you know top salespeople will be. Commit to attending three to five of these events over the next year.

4. Build relationships with top salespeople in your field.

When you discover top performers in your industry, reach out. Don't put the hard sell on them; simply congratulate them on their recent accomplishments and start to form a relationship.

Remember, this is about developing ongoing relationships with superstar salespeople. The best DIY recruiters are constantly out there building these relationships, and it's a top priority.

THE POWER OF DIY RECRUITING: CASE STUDY

One of my friends is the CEO of a large regional real estate firm in New England. Several years ago, she decided to recruit her team all by herself—one by one. Today, her company does $1 billion in transactions every year.

One of the reasons she's had so much success is that she made it a priority to focus on recruiting the best real estate agents in particular geographies. She began meeting face-to-face with three potential agents each week. As a result of this strategy, she was able to grow her firm from 100 reps to 300 reps in just two years, and dramatically increase the performance level of her team.

5. Send customized LinkedIn messages.

Intentional, personalized LinkedIn messages are a top strategy for recruiting sales talent. Credit for this approach goes to my friend Mark Roberge, former chief revenue officer at HubSpot. He shared this LinkedIn recruiting approach with me, and now I share it with my clients. Why? Because it works.

LinkedIn messages with "soft asks" that come from a senior company leader always catch the attention of salespeople. Roberge sent out these messages every day when he was first starting to build sales at HubSpot. You can do it a couple of times a week—and you can even outsource the process.

Give your LinkedIn account information to an assistant, and have the assistant send customized messages to high-level salespeople a few times a week. Reference the salesperson's company, college, hometown, mutual contacts, and anything else relevant that might make a connection. Here's an example:

Email Subject: Halo / Wisconsin College
Email Body:
Nancy,

Congratulations on all of your success in sales! I own Marc Wayshak Sales Research & Insights. Our processes have become so dialed in that we are focused exclusively on expanding the team. Your background seems similar to that of our other top performers.

Do you know of any folks in your network who might be in the job market and have a similar background to yours?

Best,

Marc Wayshak

CEO of Marc Wayshak Sales Research & Insights

6. Keep an eye on your company's Glassdoor.com reviews.

Glassdoor.com is like the Yelp or TripAdvisor for companies. It's a place where employees, as well as candidates who have gone through your hiring process, can write anonymous reviews about your organization. Glassdoor can be a major source of blood loss for companies—but they don't even realize it most of the time.

No matter how much time and effort you put into recruiting people, once they check Glassdoor and find horrible reviews of your company, it's all over.

If you haven't yet, set up a free profile and read your reviews. Do the reviews of your company paint a positive story? We all know that every organization has had a disgruntled employee or two, or even someone who went through the hiring process only to not get the job. These people can write damaging reviews that stick with your company for a very long time. You're not alone if you find some surprising feedback about your company at Glassdoor. What matters is that you engage with your reviews and work to improve your ratings.

Glassdoor can be a major source of blood loss for companies—but they don't even realize it most of the time.

One of my former client companies, a large services provider, had terrible reviews on Glassdoor— but they were actually old reviews from when the company was under completely different management. Instead of engaging with those outdated reviews, they were just ignoring them. The worst part was that the reviews had absolutely nothing to do with the current company, but they were still causing massive brand damage.

This is why it's so important to respond to every single review on your Glassdoor profile, whether good or bad. Ideally, you yourself should respond, not someone in HR. Think about the powerful message it sends for potential candidates to see that the CEO or VP of sales personally responds to any feedback about the company.

Here are several key ways to make sure your Glassdoor profile is working in your favor:

- Ask happy employees to write their honest reviews on Glassdoor

- Respond to negative reviews without being defensive

- Take ownership of your company's page and check it regularly

- If you see legitimate issues being raised in the reviews, make sure you address them within your organization

Remember, almost every single person who applies for a job at your company is going to check your Glassdoor page. Make sure it leaves a positive impression.

7. Write job descriptions for superstars.

Throughout this chapter, we've repeatedly established that recruiting and hiring A player salespeople is a sales leadership function, not an HR function. The same is true about writing job descriptions. In fact, job descriptions shouldn't be HR documents at all, although they're widely considered to be. In reality, job descriptions are marketing pieces.

Hear me out. A job description can be used as a template for the position, but it's also a message to the world. That means it's picked up by outside recruiters, used in online job postings, shared to social media and job boards, and distributed to your organization's employees. It's a living, breathing document that should market the heck out of the position you're trying to fill.

You can always tell when a job description has been written as an HR document because it doesn't market the job. It's clinical, boring, and just gives a barebones description of what the job requires. These job descriptions never give a full-color account of what it's like to work for the company, or why superstars should be rushing to apply.

To give you an idea of what I mean, below is a portion of a job description from a client of mine, written by the director of HR:

JOB PROFILE

The Account Executive position requires an individual that is both self-starter and self-motivated; someone who can identify, qualify, and convert sales leads into lifelong company clients, through the use of effective communications and strong relationship building skills. A successful Account Executive is able to easily multi-task; is very organized; well prepared and always dependable. An effective Account Executive is some-one who grasps an understanding of employer and client objectives and seeks to exceed both the employer's and the client's expectations. An individual with these skill sets will be both confident and competent in the role of Account Executive.

Remember, you're trying to *market* this job! The job description above, besides being tedious to read, would also make superstars run the other way.

There's nothing unique or specific about the job described here. Instead, the "Account Executive" sounds like the most general, unspecified role possible, with virtually no defining characteristics. In addition, there's no information about the company itself. Referring to itself as "the employer," the hiring company shoots itself in the foot yet again by presenting as a stiff, boring, and totally original place to work.

Now that you know what *not to do,* here are the six keys to writing job descriptions that actually attract superstar talent:

1. Engage and stand out.

We tell our salespeople to stand out from other salespeople when they interact with prospects. We tell them to truly engage the prospect, think from the prospect's perspective, and avoid sounding like everyone else. Well, the same is true about writing job descriptions. You need to stand out from competing job descriptions and work to actively engage your ideal candidates.

The best way to do this is to put yourself in the shoes of a top-performing salesperson in your industry. This person sees job descriptions all the time—so how will yours stand out? Think about what *you* would want to see in a job posting.

One thing we can all agree on: An engaging, conversational tone that makes it clear you're hearing from an actual human being. Most job descriptions are filled to the brim with soulless business-speak. Stand out right away by being more casual in your language, addressing the reader as a real, full-blooded person who's looking to find a particular experience.

2. **Tell your company story from the first person.**

In the very first paragraph of your job description, tell your company story from the first person. This is a personal touch that draws candidates in, while giving them an insider's view of what's special about your organization. Any great salesperson is going to want the inside scoop before applying to your company, so this is a surefire way to appeal to A players from the get-go.

Remember, this isn't an essay about your company origins. Rather, it's a short paragraph about your organization, and what's so great about working there. We'll get to some examples in just a minute.

3. Challenge applicants.

Use language in your job description that challenges applicants. Show them that—if they're up for a challenge and willing to do what it takes—they'll be successful at your organization. Be clear that you're only looking for top performers who are willing to roll up their sleeves, do the work, and prove that they're superstars.

4. Lay out exactly what the candidate will do in the job.

This is pretty straightforward. Be detailed about what the job requires. Lay out what the salesperson will be doing day to day, week to week, and month to month.

5. Appeal to A players, not B players.

How? Explicitly say that you're only looking for A players, not B players—and that B players will struggle at the job. It really is that simple.

6. Clarify Must-haves vs. Wants.

Make sure your job description is clear about what's required versus what's desired. Include up to five Must-haves in your job description, and up to four Wants.

Here's a great placement ad that you can emulate as you write your own:

LOOKING FOR A SALES SUPERSTAR – WEALTH ASSOCIATE, NEW YORK, NY

We're looking for an overachiever who will become our next sales superstar.

XYZ Company, a leading financial services organization for the New York City area, seeks a sales professional to add to its rapidly growing and highly successful sales team. We think we're pretty awesome. Our mission is to provide financial solutions to navigate the journey of life. XYZ Company exists to improve the lives of our members, employees, and communities.

We foster a family environment that supports and celebrates the success of our team. In turn, this creates an amazing culture for our employees. We provide our salespeople with a massive suite of products and services to improve the lives of our clients, while creating great opportunities to grow a book of business.

We don't hire backgrounds. If you're average, you'll be uncomfortable here. But if you're a superstar, you'll thrive here. This is an outstanding opportunity to not only create great financial success for our clients, but also for yourself. We fully intend to support candidates who are willing to put in the effort to build a book of business. We will also invest aggressively to help you learn all critical skills and obtain all necessary licenses.

XYZ Company is currently seeking a wealth associate who will provide financial solutions to our clients. This requires the ability to develop deep and meaningful relationships with those who are just starting their financial journey, as well as with high-net worth individuals.

Main responsibilities include:
- Making outbound sales calls to prospective clients on a daily basis
- Following a structured sales process to profile and qualify prospective clients
- Networking and creating partnerships with other departments to obtain and provide appropriately qualified referrals
- Scheduling quality appointments for senior advisors who will help close larger or more complex opportunities
- Responding to inbound leads and fielding web inquiries

The successful candidate must be:
- A self-starter who is willing to make over 100 dials each day
- Mentally tough and willing to take regular rejection
- Consistent in performing measurable and effective sales behaviors
- Highly coachable and able to implement feedback from managers and team leaders
- Detail-oriented and organized with excellent follow-up skills

WARNING: You should only apply if you view yourself as a sales hunter! We need you to consistently perform sales behaviors. What's in it for you is a career path that can lead to outstanding personal financial success.

The successful candidate must have:
- 2-3 years of successful sales experience
- A college degree or equivalent mix of education and experience
- Excellent computer skills
- The ability to travel around the New York City area

If you're looking for a tremendous opportunity to work on a rapidly growing sales team, send your resume to [EMAIL].

For other examples of strong placement ads, Google the following terms: HubSpot Sales Job and Salesforce.com Sales Job.

HIRING AN OUTSIDE RECRUITER

Now you have a clear path to building your own DIY recruiting strategy, from networking to writing job descriptions. But what if you want to turn up the volume?

When I first sit down with CEOs to lay out hiring strategy for top sales talent, they usually tell me they've worked with recruiters in the past. More often than not, those recruiters were really expensive, and led my clients to hire people who didn't end up working out. So, my clients tell me they don't want to use a recruiter ever again. This is usually the fault of weak profiles and hiring processes.

However, if you really need new talent at your organization, and you want lots of new leads coming into your pipeline on a regular basis, then recruiters can be a great resource. Notwithstanding your past experience with recruiters, I promise you can find one that works for you.

If you implement a strong, tough hiring process, you're far less likely to waste money on recruiting fees, because you simply won't hire the wrong people.

As far as the cost, it's more of a question of math than anything else. If a good hire becomes your top salesperson, how much money will that person bring into your organization? Take a look at what your current top-performing salesperson has earned for your organization over the past three to five years. Chances are, it's a lot of money. Whatever it is, that's what a new hire is worth to your organization. And that's the value of a good recruiter.

The secret to finding a good recruiter actually lies in your organization's hiring process, which we'll discuss in the next chapter. Most organizations have bad experiences with recruiters because their own internal hiring processes are disorganized and weak. In other words, the recruiter isn't the problem. The hiring process is. If you implement a strong, tough hiring process, you're far less likely to waste money on recruiting fees, because you simply won't hire the wrong people.

Before we talk more about how to work successfully with recruiters, let's cover the four main types of recruiters out there:

1. Generalists (avoid them)

2. Recruiters who specialize in your industry

3. Recruiters who specialize in sales talent

4. Local recruiters who specialize in your geographic area

If you're like most executives, then you're looking for a combination of at least two of the elements above. You might be looking for sales talent with experience in your specific industry. Or, sales talent within your specific geographic location. The first step to finding the right recruiter is determining what's most important to you. You can rarely find a recruiter who specializes in all three—your industry, and sales talent, and your geographic area. Be prepared to compromise.

HOW TO WORK WITH A RECRUITER

Once you identify a recruiter with the right specialization, you need to follow a clear strategy to work together. My number one rule with recruiters is to work with them on a contingency basis.

There are two ways to work with recruiters: on contingency and on retainer. Contingency means you only pay them upon successfully hiring someone. Retainer means you pay them a fee up front just for looking for talent. Never work with recruiters completely on retainer. If you have to pay some money up front, that's fine, but make sure that most of the upside is contingent upon placing a hire who stays around for at least 90 days. No exceptions.

Here are two other rules to follow when working with recruiters:

1. **Reward recruiters generously.**

   Always reward recruiters generously when they find you a good hire. The industry standard is anywhere from 15% to 25% of the new hire's expected compensation for the first year. If the recruiter is willing to guarantee it's the right person for the job, then 25% of the first year's expected compensation is totally reasonable.

2. **Build ongoing relationships with recruiters.**

   Recruiters can be a great resource for you—and you're a great client for them. It's a win-win situation when a company matches with a great recruiter. Be sure to keep that relationship alive by checking in regularly.

As I said before, much of your success with recruiters will depend on the strength of your hiring process. Recruiting is only the first part of the conversation about attracting top talent to your organization. Ultimately, you must have a rock-solid strategy for hiring the right people once they come knocking on your door—and sending the wrong people on their way. That's exactly what we'll cover in the following chapter.

Chapter 4:

The Hiring Process

WE'VE COVERED A lot of ground already when it comes to attracting top talent. The natural next step is to explore how to successfully hire those top performers.

The most important component of any hiring process is an effective system of knowing when you're in front of a true top performer. Otherwise, you'll keep making bad hires and letting superstars slip away. This happens far too often, as half of all candidates get the job based on the hiring manager's "gut feel" that the candidate "had what it took" to succeed in the job.[38]

We can talk all day about how to source great candidates for your sales jobs. But it's just as crucial that you have a repeatable method to confidently determine whether someone is a top performer.

One of the main reasons that companies don't consistently hire is that they've been burned by the hiring process so many times before. Executives often tell me they feel like they waste valuable time when trying to fill an open position. They're not wrong: The average time to replace a sales hire ranges from 3.69 months for inside sales to 5.42 months for field sales.[39]

In this chapter, you'll learn how to avoid making mis-hires by using a systematic hiring process that dramatically lowers hiring risk.

But first, let's take a look at two of the most common hiring pitfalls out there: unstructured interviews and overreliance on past results. We'll address these hiring traps before we lay out your new and improved hiring process.

THE DANGER OF UNSTRUCTURED INTERVIEWS

The vast majority of organizations rely on unstructured interviews as the central determining factor of whether to hire someone. Simply put, these wildly popular unstructured interviews are a trap. Countless studies have shown that they're not only ineffective at determining future success at a job, but they can also be a significantly lower predictor than *never having met the person at all.*

The average time to replace a sales hire ranges from 3.69 months for inside sales to 5.42 months for field sales.

Think about that for a minute. It's mind-blowing.

A great deal of research has been done on this point. In a 2012 study, researchers at the University of Pennsylvania found that interviewers made significantly more accurate predictions about the G.P.A.s of students they had never met, based purely on their course schedules and past G.P.As., than those they had interviewed. The same researchers found that interviewers will make sense of virtually anything an interviewee says in an unstructured interview, regardless of its actual validity.

This is called "sensemaking" and it's a very real problem in the hiring world. In the U Penn study, one group of interviewees answered questions according to a random system, while the other group answered honestly. Interviewers couldn't tell the difference. The researchers' conclusion? "Impressions formed from unstructured interviews can seem valid and inspire confidence even when interviews are useless. Our simple recommendation…is not to use them."[40]

Another study published in the *Psychological Bulletin* found that unstructured interviews alone only give you an 8% likelihood of being able to predict a candidate's success.[41] That's terrible. What's even worse is that, for most organizations, these unstructured interviews make up almost the entire hiring process. Often, the candidate's past results are the only other factor considered.

> *What you don't know can hurt you.*

THE HEURISTICS OF PAST RESULTS

As you might have guessed, past results aren't a strong predictor of job success, either. Even if a candidate tells the truth on his or her resumé, you can never assume it's the whole truth. Candidates smartly pick and choose what to highlight on their resumés. They only share past results that feed into a positive narrative about their work experience. What you don't know can hurt you.

Take the example of Corey, a top-performing salesperson at one of my recent client companies. Corey pulled in $4.2 million in sales, when the average on the team was just $1 million. If you interviewed Corey for a position at your company, you'd look at his past results and conclude he was a superstar. Right?

Wrong. The numbers don't tell the whole story. The whole story is that Corey had been at the company for 15 years. Everyone else on the team was relatively new, having joined within the past two to five years. As a result, Corey had the biggest book of business—by far. He won the war of attrition, so to speak. Corey just stuck around the longest, and his "results" had very little to do with his actual ability. If you asked his manager, he'd tell you Corey was a B- performer.

I can predict this: When Corey ultimately goes looking for a new job, he'll trick his next employer into thinking he's a top performer deserving of a huge salary. In fact, he's not. Corey isn't hard-working or ambitious. He never gets face-to-face with his clients and he often rubs people the wrong way. May Corey's story be a warning to executives everywhere.

If you follow the hiring process I'm about to show you, you'll avoid hiring the Coreys of the world. I'll show you how to identify those sneaky candidates who present well in unstructured interviews, but who will ultimately turn out to be under-performers on your team.

These salespeople are everywhere. They're smooth talkers, they dress well, and they look you in the eye with a charming, self-assured smile. But when it comes down to it, they're wolves in sheep's clothing. They won't work hard, and they don't have the ability to think strategically.

If you stick to this hiring process with every candidate, you'll avoid hiring one of these salespeople. What's more, you'll be able to compare apples to apples when comparing different candidates, giving you a real sense of confidence when choosing who to hire. Let's begin.

YOUR NEW HIRING PROCESS

Every single step of this process is highly structured, scripted, and not a place for you to improvise or get creative. Follow the system. Here we go:

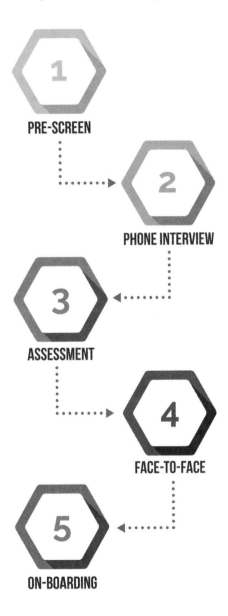

1. Pre-Screen

One of the biggest reasons why companies are resistant to hiring is that it's time-consuming. The pre-screen is a tool that cuts your hiring process time in half. It does this by removing 50% of your candidates up front, "screening" every reasonable candidate with a highly structured seven-minute pre-screen phone call. When you start your hiring process with the pre-screen, you can know with confidence that candidates you eliminate up front would never have been effective on your sales team.

Here's the central idea behind the pre-screen: Sales is the only job category where you can use the interview process to test someone's ability to do the actual job in question. If you hire someone for an operations role, you can't use an interview to test the candidate's operational ability. With sales, on the other hand, you can test the candidate's selling ability through the interview process.

The pre-screen is your opportunity to test every candidate's actual selling ability. Let's say you put out a placement ad, hire a recruiter, or do whatever else works for you to get 20 acceptable resumés in your hands. You sort through the resumés and filter for the candidates that generally fit your Ideal Candidate Profile. You find 10 that are a fit.

> *Sales is the only job category where you can use the interview process to test someone's ability to do the actual job in question.*

At this point, most companies would normally go straight to setting up 10 face-to-face unstructured interviews. This requires many hours of management work and, as we already established, unstructured interviews are useless anyway.

Instead, we want to avoid taking this rash step. That's where the pre-screen comes in:

1. **Set up a seven-minute phone call with each of your 10 candidates.** The easiest way to do this is to block off three different one-hour windows over the course of a week. For example, Monday at 10 am, Wednesday at 4 pm, and Thursday at 12 pm.

   Have an administrator send out an email to each of your 10 candidates that looks like this:

EMAIL TO SET UP PRE-SCREEN

Email Subject: Sales Position Phone Interview for COMPANY NAME

Email Body:

Hi NAME,

Thanks so much for applying for the sales representative role at COMPANY NAME. After reviewing your resumé, we would like to set up a brief initial phone interview with you. The call will take no more than 10 minutes. We'd ask that you pick one of three windows of time for the call. This means we will call you at some point during the chosen window. The three windows of time are:

OPTION 1 _____

OPTION 2 _____

OPTION 3 _____

Which of these three windows works best for you? Again, we will call you at some point during your chosen window, so please keep the entire window of time available. Really looking forward to our call.

Thanks so much,

YOUR NAME

This allows you to have each candidate waiting by the phone, so you or a sales manager (but not HR) can do the interviews back-to-back. Of course, if you only end up having two or three good candidates for a job, you won't need to do this. But for the sake of this example, you've got 10, so you have to be smart about scheduling. If you schedule 10 seven-minute calls at different times, on different days—well, it'll be a long, slow process. The pre-screen should be quick.

2. **For each seven-minute phone call, create a Word doc so you can take copious notes throughout the call.** When you're ready to begin, follow this script:

    -   **"What do you know about our company?"** The best sales candidates will have done research and spent time preparing for this interview.

    -   **"What do you know about me?"** You can tell a great deal about a salesperson from the answer to this question. What does the candidate know about the person who is conducting the interview? Any good sales candidates who care about the job will have done initial research on your LinkedIn profile, looked up your bio on the company site, etc. That's why the answer to this question gives you insight into the candidate's approach as a salesperson.

    -   **"The ad said not to apply unless you're a superstar. So tell me, why should we interview you?"** Make sure the candidate responds to this question and gives you an answer. The specifics of what he or she says aren't important. What matters is that the candidate pushes back. Any veteran salesperson can tell you about exceeding annual sales goals, but what you're really looking for here is *fight*.

- **"I'm not really hearing it."** Regardless of what the candidate said in response to the previous question, you should then respond with: "I'm not really hearing it."

> *You're using this interview process to assess the salesperson's actual ability to handle tough prospects.*

- **"I'm *still* not really hearing it."** Say it again, after giving the candidate a chance to respond. This should be uncomfortable both for you and the candidate. You're giving a little bit of rejection and pushback. It's important not to be mean or highly confrontational here. Just be matter-of-fact. What should this conversation start to feel like? A tough sales call. The question at this point is: Does the candidate push back—or does the candidate rush to get off the phone?

  You want to see how the salesperson handles rejection up front. Hopefully, you can see how you're using this interview process to assess the salesperson's actual ability to handle tough prospects. As I said before, the specifics of what the candidate says are much less important than the fact that he or she pushes back and takes a stand.

- **"That sounds great. That makes a lot of sense. Thank you for saying that."** Always cognizant of Glassdoor.com ratings, we get gentle here. Plus, we want to ultimately build a relationship with the candidate.

- **"What are your career goals?"** A gentler question to end the interview on a softer note.

- **"Who were your last three bosses, and how will each of them rate your performance on a 1 to 10 scale when we talk to them?"** This question acts like truth serum. The candidates know you're going to talk to their former bosses directly, so they're compelled to give you honest answers. If a candidate answers with anything under 8, it's a red flag.

3. **At the end of each pre-screen interview, refer back to your Word doc and review your notes. Give each candidate a 1–10 rating.** Candidates who come out of this call with less than a 7 rating will not be moving forward in the hiring process. Use your gut to rate each candidate and don't second-guess yourself. Anyone who gets a 7 or above will move on to the next step in the hiring process.

The fact that pre-screens are done on the phone is highly intentional. Getting face-to-face with candidates—even through Skype—leads to immediate biases in the way we perceive them. The minute you look someone in the eye, you're no longer purely objective about the decisions you make.

In fact, a study published in *Psychological Science* showed that people make lasting judgments about traits such as likeability, trustworthiness, and competence after just 100 milliseconds of exposure to a stranger's face.[42] Use the pre-screen religiously to avoid making biased decisions and you'll eliminate 50% of your candidates right out the gate.

2. Full Phone Interview

The second step of your new hiring process is the full phone interview. This is a highly structured, scripted interview that should take between 30 and 45 minutes to complete. Just as you did in the pre-screen, you'll be taking copious notes throughout these phone interviews, and ultimately giving each candidate a rating between 1 and 10. Anyone under a 7 is immediately disqualified from the hiring process, while 7s and above will move on to the next phase.

Follow this script during each phone interview:

1. Tell me more about your career goals.

2. Why are you leaving your current job?

3. What do you want in your next job?

4. How do you feel about sales?

5. How do you feel about prospecting to new people?

6. What was the toughest sale you ever made?

7. Tell me about a time when the odds were stacked against you and you overcame.

8. What kind of money do you want to make?
   - Within 1 year?

9. How committed are you to moving on?

10. What are you good at professionally?

- What are you not good at or not interested in doing professionally?

11. I know I asked this before, but who were your last three bosses, and how will they each rate your performance on a 1–10 scale when we talk to them?

12. We'll get back to you if we decide to move forward. (See if the candidate asks about next steps—this shows strong sales initiative.)

3. Online Assessment

This assessment is the only part of the hiring process that uses purely objective data to help you make the right hiring decision. We've talked about creating your own Ideal Candidate Profile based on your wants and needs. But the online assessment is your opportunity to use hard data to help you measure candidates in a wide range of areas relevant to sales.

While the results of the online assessment should make up less than a third of your ultimate hiring decision, it's an incredibly helpful tool for understanding your candidates' current skills and future potential.

There are thousands of online assessments available. The one I recommend, and have used for years with my own clients, is from Profiles International (PI). To learn more about it, you can visit the PI website and fill out an interest form.

This assessment is about 75 minutes long and full of SAT-style questions, as well as behavioral and interest-based questions. At the end of each test, PI provides a printable report detailing the outcomes so you can easily review candidates' results. In addition, the assessment generates a useful "interview question guide," giving you the best questions to ask candidates later on, should they progress to the next step in the hiring process.

Because millions of people have taken the PI assessment, there's a tremendous amount of data that allows us to draw reliable conclusions from the assessment results. In addition, PI measures three key areas that I've found to be important predictors of job success:

1. Cognitive ability

2. Behaviors and personality

3. Interests and motivations

These three areas are critical to understanding the likelihood that a candidate will be successful at a job. Keep in mind, though, that we want to be careful about generalizing all salespeople when it comes to the details of these traits.

The online assessment is your opportunity to use hard data to help you measure candidates in a wide range of areas relevant to sales.

If you're reading this book, it's safe to assume that you're looking for more consultative salespeople. Based on that assumption, let's take a look at some of the traits you'll want to look for in any assessment you choose.

After assessing thousands of salespeople—and hundreds of top performers—via the PI assessment, my data shows that there are six traits that are the most highly correlated with selling success. That is to say, if a candidate scores *within the right parameters* in these six areas, it tends to suggest that that person is at least likely to be successful in sales.

It's important to note that most people generally fit in the middle, with regards to any of the traits you see below. On a 1 to 10 scale, that means the vast majority of people fall between a 4 and a 7 (essentially, within 1 standard deviation). While we have a tendency to think that more of any trait is always better, that's not always true, as we discussed earlier.

1. **Cognitive ability.**

   Few organizations measure the cognitive ability of their employees. But recent data suggests that cognitive ability is actually the top measurable predictor of job performance.[43] In fact, it's a stronger indicator than personality, behavior, interests, and motivations.

   Cognitive ability refers to verbal ability, math ability, and the ability to think strategically. In sales, this is particularly crucial. Hardly anyone uses a "one-call close" approach in sales anymore. Instead, selling is much more nuanced, requiring multiple steps, and the ability to think strategically through a complex selling situation.

   Another manifestation of cognitive ability is the salesperson's ability to understand and retain new ideas in sales. That's why it's incredibly important to measure cognitive ability in every candidate you consider for a sales job. On a scale from 1 to 10, with 10 being the highest level of cognitive ability, the sweet spot for salespeople is somewhere in the 6 to 9 range.

Cognitive ability is actually the top measurable predictor of job performance.

Below a 6, salespeople have issues selling strategically and they're unable to effectively learn about the offering. What's less obvious is that 10s can get easily bored with sales jobs, which often require consistent repetition. That's why 10s tend to leave sales positions to go into management or entrepreneurship, seeking a wider variety of tasks and more challenging roles.

Hardly anyone uses a "one-call close" approach in sales anymore.

2. **Assertiveness.**

This one is relatively simple. You want salespeople to be assertive, but not overly domineering. A score in the 6 to 9 range is best here. These salespeople are appropriately assertive with prospects but not so much so that they roll all over prospects.

3. **Sociability.**

Most people assume that top-performing salespeople are all 10s in sociability. I call this the myth of the sales extrovert. In reality, the best salespeople aren't too sociable.

Earlier in this book, we looked at data from a study which showed that the highest performing salespeople are actually neither introverts nor extroverts, but rather ambiverts, whose personality traits fall exactly in between. In the study, these ambiverts blew their counterparts out of the water, earning nearly 60% more than both introverts and extroverts did.[44]

So it's important to recognize that top-performing salespeople may score higher in the area of sociability, but not too high. The sweet spot is that 5 to 8 range, once again. When salespeople are a 10, they tend to get distracted by making friends instead of focusing on selling.

4. Accommodating.

The best salespeople score lower in this trait—but they shouldn't be 1s, because 1s are typically difficult to deal with. A small element of accommodation may be required to make nuanced deals with high-level prospects. But salespeople aren't customer service people, either. The ideal range here is 2 to 4.

5. Manageability.

The sweet spot for manageability is smack dab in the middle: 4 to 6. Top-performing salespeople aren't looking to have their hands held, but they're also not challenging, recalcitrant employees.

6. Independence.

Independence is a trait that largely depends on the type of role your salesperson will fill. If a salesperson is going to work virtually with very little management, you might want a 9. But if your salesperson will be working in a group environment and reporting to managers, then a 7 might be more your speed. Use your own judgment here. Different industries, sale sizes, company cultures, and management structures can all influence the ideal independence rating.

Here's a graph to help you visualize what we just discussed. These are the averages of the 6 traits for 50 top performers I've assessed over the years:

TOP TRAIT SCORES

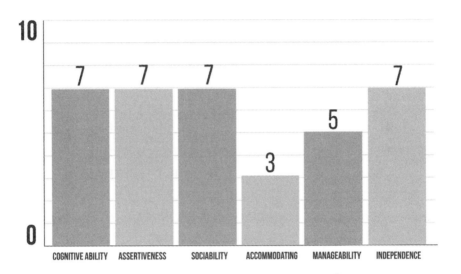

If you already have an assessment in place, great. Just make sure it measures cognitive ability and doesn't use generic sales models as benchmarks. This may require adding an additional assessment to your existing program. If you don't have an assessment in place already, start using the PI assessment. For my own clients, I create performance models using existing data that I have of top performers in their industry, or by using data from specific top performers currently on their sales team.

4. Face-to-Face Interview

By waiting to do the face-to-face interview until this point in the hiring process, you're avoiding the bias that inevitably becomes a problem when you meet candidates too early in the game. Nearly half of all recruiters say that just seeing a picture of candidates before meeting them influences their first impression.[45]

Instead, you're using real, hard data up front to determine who's a good fit for the open position, before ever laying eyes on your candidates. By taking this approach, you also cut down the number of face-to-face interviews you need to do—usually by more than half. While normally companies conduct at least 10 face-to-face interviews for one job, only about three people typically make it to the face-to-face interview portion of this hiring process. That's a lot of management time saved.

Now, this four-part face-to-face interview does require some prep on your part. For each interview, it's important to put aside at least 15 minutes to prepare the questions you'll ask each candidate. It might sound like a lot, but this time pays off. Preparing the right questions will help you better understand whether a candidate is the right person for the job.

Nearly half of all recruiters say that just seeing a picture of candidates before meeting them influences their first impression.

Here are the four parts to the interview:

1. **Address any concerns or questions that arose during your phone interview with the candidate.**

   Even the strongest candidates have some potential areas of concern. In fact, I can't recall a single phone interview with a candidate that didn't leave me with at least one question or some need for clarification.

Look back at your notes for each candidate, review the resumé, and bring up any concerns at the start of this face-to-face interview.

A good tip is to think about whether there are any holes in the candidate's story. Come up with three specific questions you have from the phone interview, write them out, and have them ready to go at the beginning of the face-to-face interview. Think like a detective playing bad-cop.

2. Ask four questions from the online assessment interview question guide.

Remember how the online assessment generates questions for you to ask candidates in interviews further down the road? Well, now you've arrived further down the road. Take that assessment interview guide and pull out the four questions most relevant to the concerns you have about the candidate.

An example might be that your candidate scored very high on the "accommodating" trait. (Remember, "high" doesn't mean "good.") This means they're likely to go with the flow. So, your interview guide may prompt you to ask: "Can you tell me about a time when you had a client who pushed back with a completely unreasonable demand on price, product, or service? How did you handle that situation?"

3. Dig into their last three relevant jobs.

Again, think of yourself as a detective. Ask for clarification on any vague statements about past jobs or employers, and make sure candidates explain what they mean. For example, if a candidate says, "I left my last job because my boss and I didn't see eye-to-eye," press for more details. Here are some specific questions to ask:

"What did you do at your last job?"

"What was your greatest accomplishment while in that position?"

"What was your toughest experience at that job?"

"Who was your boss at that job, and what was it like working for that person?"

"What will that boss say were your biggest strengths, and your areas for improvement?"

"Why did you leave that job?"

4. Role play.

This is one of the most important parts of the interview. The role play is an opportunity for candidates to demonstrate their sales ability in real-time. Give candidates the chance to conduct a 10-minute discovery conversation with you. Pretend you're on the phone, or let it be a face-to-face selling situation. You're the prospect, and your candidate is the salesperson. Stop at the 10-minute mark, no matter where you are in the conversation. See how they do.

The role play is an opportunity for candidates to demonstrate their sales ability in real-time.

This four-part face-to-face interview should last no more than 90 minutes total. Be disciplined about your time and move the interview along at a good pace. Just because an interview goes long, that doesn't mean it was good. It just shows bad discipline on your part as the interviewer.

5. Reference Interview

The reference interview is an area where many organizations tend to take short-cuts. The reason for this is quite obvious: Once they've decided that they like a candidate, they don't want to find information that will dissuade them from making the decision to hire that person. But in truth, the entire hiring process is about disqualifying candidates.

If you can get information from an outsider who can provide you with insight into a candidate, it would be delinquent not to consider that information. It's important to note that you don't just want any references. You don't want peer-to-peer or friend references, for example, as they're hand-picked to say nice things. You should only consider references from relatively recent past employers.

Here's a scripted interview you can use, word-for-word, when talking to a reference:

1. In what capacity did you work with CANDIDATE?

2. What were CANDIDATE's biggest strengths?

3. Back when CANDIDATE worked for you, what were his/her biggest areas for improvement?

4. On a 1 to 10 scale, how would you rate CANDIDATE'S overall performance on the job? What about his/her performance caused you to choose that rating?

5. CANDIDATE mentioned that he/she struggled with
_____ in that job. Can you tell me a little more
about that?

6. Onboarding

Onboarding is one of the most critical pieces of the hiring
process, but many companies overlook it. When organizations make a hiring decision, they usually put very little
thought into how to get that person up and running in the
position. But in reality, the average sales rep takes over
four months to ramp up at the job, despite spending less
than three years in the position.[46] It's crucial that you begin to think about onboarding as part of the hiring process, and not as something separate.

In fact, research shows that effective onboarding leads
to more profit growth and better sales results. Firms with
strong onboarding programs achieve 14% better results in
sales and profit objective achievement, and 10% greater
sales growth rates.[47]

During the first 90 days at their new jobs, salespeople are
really in a trial period. It's a trial period for the salesperson to
see if he or she likes the company, and
for the company to see if they think
the salesperson is going to make it.
Studies show that 18% of high-performing sales organizations will
terminate under-performing reps
within 90 days compared to only 2% of
average-performing organizations.[48]
So, this 90-day period is still very

> *The average sales rep
> takes over four months
> to ramp up at the
> job, despite spending
> less than three years
> in the position.*

much a part of your active hiring process; it doesn't just end once the person is hired. (Plus, if you've recruited someone, you'll want to know whether that person is a fit within the first 90 days, since that's typically the guarantee period for recruiters.)

> *While hiring multiple salespeople at once isn't for everyone, use it to your advantage when it makes sense for your business.*

This is why it's so important to implement a highly structured, effective onboarding process. When hiring just one person at a time, many companies struggle with this. It's far easier to be structured about onboarding when hiring multiple people at once, for reasons that quickly become obvious. If a company typically hires multiple salespeople every quarter or so, it forces leadership to think about how to onboard them in a systematic, group-minded way.

I had a recent client who took this approach. They're a merchant processor who would hire four to six new salespeople every quarter and enroll them in onboarding classes. This forced them to think about the onboarding process in a very systematic way. As a result, new recruits were up and running in under two months.

On the other hand, hiring just one person at a time can be haphazard. There's no pressure to design a class for just one person, and so the new hire can quickly become forgotten in terms of training. While hiring multiple salespeople at once isn't for everyone, use it to your advantage when it makes sense for your business. It simply forces you to be more systematic and to create more organization around onboarding.

Whether you hire just one salesperson or 10 of them, there are two critical elements to onboarding:

1. **Create a formal schedule for the first four weeks on the job.** Each weekly schedule can look something like this:

	Monday	Tuesday	Wednesday	Thursday	Friday
8:00 AM					
9:00 AM	Arrival & Set-Up	Salesforce Basics	Meet with Project Manager	Meet with Consultant	Sales Team 1:1s
10:00 AM	Meet with IT - Workspace	Meet with CFO	Meet with Auditing Department	Client Meeting	
11:00 AM	Office Tour	Listen In on Sales Calls	Meet with VP of Marketing	First Sales Calls	
12:00 PM	Lunch with Sales Team	Hold for Lunch	Hold for Lunch	Hold for Lunch	Lunch with CEO
1:00 PM		Meet with Director of Operations	Client Meeting	Sales Calls Review with Team Leader	
2:00 PM	Weekly Sales Team Meeting	Sales Process Review	Meet with EVP of Strategy	Meet with Creative Department	Sales Team 1:1s
3:00 PM	Meet with HR	Meet with Sales Administrators	Meet with Operations Manager	Meet with HR	Sales Calls
4:00 PM	Check-In w/ Sales Manager	Check-In w/ Sales Manager	Check-In w/ Sales Manager	Check-In w/ Sales Manager	Check-In w/ Sales Manager
5:00 PM					

 You can download a free PDF version of this chart in my Key Pages & Worksheets Guide at www.MarcWayshak.com/HighVelocity.

This should be a day-to-day schedule that clearly lays out what's expected of the new hire, when it's expected, and where it should happen. Make sure the CEO, president, or some other senior leader is involved in this first month of activities. Your involvement as an executive leader shows new hires that they're important to the company.

Assuming it's appropriate for the job, it's usually a good idea to get salespeople into the field as quickly as possible during that first month. Get them on the phone making calls within the first week and give them low-risk prospects that they can pursue throughout the month.

2. **Map out the first six months of the job.** Outline what will be expected of the new hire over the next six months. Here's an example:

Month One
- Week One Online Training/Developing Prospect/ Suspect List/learning about industry/Writing Script/Role Playing
- Prospect/Suspect List: 100
- Dials for Week 2, 3 & 4: 40 per day average
- Meetings: 2 per week
- Emailer/Mailings: 10 per week
- Quote/Proposals: 2 per week

Month Two:
- Prospect/Suspect List: 150 to 200
- Dials: 40 per day average
- Meetings: 2 per week
- Prospects Added: 5 per week
- Introductions Requested: 1 per day
- Emailer/Mailings: 20 per week
- Quotes/Proposals: 5 per week
- Spec Samples: 2 per month
- Networking: 4 per month
- Sales: $2,000

Month Three:

- Prospect/Suspect List maintained at 150 to 200
- Dials: 40 per day average
- Prospects Added: 5 per week
- Introductions Requests: 1 per day
- Meetings: 2 per week
- Emailer/Mailings: 20 per week
- Quotes/Proposals 10 per week
- Spec Samples: 2 per week
- Networking: 4 per month
- Sales: $5,000

Month Four:

- Prospect/Suspect List Maintained at 150 to 200
- Dials: 40 per day average
- Prospects Added: 8/week
- Introductions Requested: 1 per day
- Meetings: 3 per week
- Emailer/Mailing: 20 per week
- Quotes/Proposals: 15 per week
- Spec Samples: 2 per week
- Networking: 4 per month
- Sales: $10,000

Month Five:

- Prospect/Suspect List Maintained at 150 to 200
- Dials: 40 per day

- Prospects Added: 8/week
- Introductions Requested: 1 per day
- Meetings: 3 per week
- Emailer/Mailing: 20 per week
- Quotes/Proposals: 15 per week
- Spec Samples: 2 per week
- Networking: 4 per month
- Sales: $15,000

Month Six:
- Prospect/Suspect List Maintained at 150 to 200
- Dials: 40 per day
- Prospects Added: 8/week
- Introductions Requested: 1 per day
- Meetings: 3 per week
- Emailer/Mailing: 20 per week
- Quotes/Proposals: 15 per week
- Spec Samples: 2 per week
- Networking: 4 per month
- Sales: $15,00

Very few companies do this well, and as a result, there are no clear expectations for the first six months on the job. It becomes difficult to assess whether new hires are succeeding, and leadership hesitates to make decisions on whether to keep them around. The consequence is that many salespeople who should have been let go within the first 90 days end up sticking around for 18 months or longer.

I can't tell you the number of times I've asked salespeople, "What do you think is expected of you on a day-to-day basis?" and they respond, "I'm not sure. I'm still trying to figure out what I'm supposed to be doing." Take the time to write out those expectations so your salespeople can give you their very best.

THE FASTER, THE BETTER

Now that you've learned the entire hiring process, let's talk about speed. Moving through the hiring process as quickly and aggressively as possible will give you the highest chance of hiring the right people. Adopt a mindset toward disqualifying candidates early on. Don't second-guess yourself or drag your feet.

> *Many salespeople who should have been let go within the first 90 days end up sticking around for 18 months or longer.*

It's no wonder that lengthy hiring practices are cited as one of the top obstacles preventing organizations from increasing headcount.[49] Companies avoid hiring because it's so time-consuming, and oftentimes ineffective and frustrating.

But this new hiring process I've just shared with you is based on the idea of jealously guarding management time. I know you have so many other things to do. That's why this is the right hiring process to use, every single time.

A NOTE ON RETENTION...

The reason I'm talking about retention in a chapter on hiring is simple: Companies spend so much time and money trying to hire the right person, but without the right processes for retention to keep new hires engaged, excited, and enthusiastic about the job, it's all useless.

Sales has a problem with retention. The average sales representative stays at the same job for just 2.5 years.[50] That's it! This is part of a larger retention issue in America, where 51% of employees are considering a new job,[51] and the typical worker will change employers 11.7 times before the age of 48.[52]

Making sure your salespeople don't become part of this trend is a question of overall strategy. There is no better retention strategy than helping your salespeople crush their sales. Create a high-velocity sales organization so that A players want to stick around. The best salespeople want to work for a company where they can make the most money, help grow the organization, and participate in a dynamic work environment. One of the most important keys to retention is creating a culture where A players are happy, satisfied, and engaged. This means setting clear expectations, and not micro-managing your top salespeople.

The average sales representative stays at the same job for just 2.5 years.

When you have all of that in place, retention is no longer a day-to-day conversation about how to keep people from leaving. The problem is simply solved as a direct result of focusing on the right sales strategy. The rest of this book lays out that process.

Section II

Strategy

ALEXANDER THE GREAT: Perhaps the most famous general of all time, he led a small army of Macedonian fighters to conquer all of Asia Minor, Egypt, and the Middle East, while bringing the mighty Persian Empire to its knees. You've heard all about him. But what about his father, King Philip II of Macedon?

Philip may not have been the greatest battlefield commander of the Ancient world, but he left his son something even more valuable: the strategy that made it all possible.

Alexander's father spent nearly two decades studying the military systems of the Greek city-states surrounding Macedon. Along the way, he developed radical new processes for organizing and supplying his fledgling army. He invented more effective battle formations and groundbreaking weaponry design, transforming the small Macedonian army into a formidable, elite armed force.

But Philip's most powerful contribution to Alexander's success was his pioneering system for an all-weather, all-season army ready to do battle at any time of year. It was the world's first professional army. Other armies of the time were seasonal in nature, with men signing up for short paid campaigns during the warmer months before returning home to farm their land.

If you want your sales team to dominate the competition, you need to give them the strategy to do it.

In contrast, Philip developed a sophisticated system of rotating army placements, creating a standing army of professional soldiers paid year-round for their military service.

This revolutionary military strategy allowed Alexander to maintain his army in the field indefinitely, no matter the season. Without it, he would never have been able to lead his small army as far as the Ganges River in India, or to crush the mightiest empire in the world. Alexander the Great would have remained just an average footnote in history.

If you want your sales team to dominate the competition, you need to give them the strategy to do it. As the story of Alexander proves, a good strategy is the difference between renowned greatness and complete anonymity. Which do you choose?

Today, while so many other sales organizations are just letting their salespeople wing it, you have a massive opportunity to establish a sales strategy that will directly help your team increase sales.

Chapter 5:

Client Acquisition Strategy

EVERYONE WANTS TO increase sales. But many organizations don't get specific about how they're actually going to do it. Executives often tell me, "we need to close more sales," "we need to acquire more clients," or "we need to get in front of more people." But at the end of the day, they never do the proper math to understand exactly how to get there. That's why this chapter about client acquisition deals with a little arithmetic. It's crucial that we take this first step together to walk through the math of how to increase sales at your organization. Otherwise, it's all just abstract.

Before I introduce you to the formula that will forever change the way you view sales growth, let's talk basics. There are only three ways to increase sales at any organization:

1. Increase the conversion rate, which means salespeople are closing a higher percentage of the opportunities they get in front of.

2. Increase the average sale size.

3. Increase the prospect pipeline, which means increasing the number of actual opportunities that go into the sales funnel (both new and existing clients)—AKA, more at-bats.

When organizations think about increasing sales, they tend to zero in on one of these three strategies. The most common strategies are increasing the conversion rate and increasing the prospect pipeline. But using just one of these strategies will rarely cut it. That's why high-velocity sales organizations incorporate all three of these methods into one selling strategy, just as the definition shows:

> **high-velocity sales organization**
> *noun*
> **1.** an organization with the right performers, strategy, and infrastructure in place, allowing it to dramatically increase sales by converting **more opportunities at higher prices to more prospects.**

When you combine all three, there's a multiplicative effect on increasing sales.

This brings us to the Sales C.A.P. Formula. C.A.P. stands for **C**onversion Rate, **A**verage Sale Size, and **P**rospect Pipeline. This formula is centered on the idea that the goal is to double sales. Now, that may or may not be the goal at your organization today, but most companies would like to see sales double at some point in time. That's why doubling sales is the cornerstone for the math in the Sales C.A.P. Formula. Take a look:

2X Sales = 1.26 x C.A.P.

That's the simplified version. Here's the formula again with everything spelled out:

2X Sales =

1.26(Conversion Rate) x 1.26(Average Sale Size) x 1.26(Prospect Pipeline)

I understand that not everyone reading this book is a math whiz. But this formula is truly extraordinary, so stick with me even if math isn't your thing. While most approaches to doubling sales call for salespeople to complete near-Herculean tasks, this formula is quite the opposite. What this formula proves is that all you actually have to do to double sales is increase each of these three areas by 26%. *Just 26%.*

The math works this way because we're dealing with multiplication, not addition. Most people, upon first looking at the Sales C.A.P. Formula, assume it should add up to an increase of 73% in sales. But in reality, the multiplication leads to a 2X increase in sales.

Here's an example. There's a services company whose salespeople close around 10% of all the opportunities they get in front of. The average sale size is $1 million, and the sales team gets in front of 100 opportunities per year. The company has $10 million in annual revenue. Most companies would try to double sales by doubling leads or conversions. But instead, let's use the Sales C.A.P. Formula to understand what this company has to do in order to double sales and achieve $20M in revenues:

2X Sales =

1.26(Conversion Rate) This means that instead of closing 10% of opportunities, the salespeople need to increase the close rate by 26%—to 12.6%.

x

1.26(Average Sale Size) The average sale size needs to increase by 26%, from $1 million to $1.26 million.

x

1.26(Prospect Pipeline) Lastly, the number of opportunities in the pipeline (both new and existing clients) needs to increase by 26%, from 100 to 126 per year.

As you're reading the above formula, you're probably noticing that none of these three tasks are particularly Herculean. Instead, they're completely reasonable. Despite the attainability of these numbers, the company's annual revenues will double by implementing this process. Here's what it will look like:

12.6% Conversion Rate

x

$1.26 million Average Sale Size

x

126 Prospect Pipeline Opportunities

=

$20 million annual revenues ($20,003,760 to be exact)

This is the best way to think about sales strategy. It's not about exploding your conversion rate, getting in front of five times the number of prospects, or doubling your average transaction size. It's about making small, manageable tweaks that provide meaningful growth in different areas of the sales process. When taken together, these relatively small changes create dramatic top-line results through the multiplicative process shown above.

The Sales C.A.P. Formula can be shifted around to address the specific goals of your organization. For example, if your goal isn't to double sales, but rather to increase sales by 50%, all you have to do is increase each area by 15% instead of 26%. Ultimately, increasing sales is all about the math. Think about what that math should look like for your organization in order to achieve your goals for sales growth over the next year.

It's about making small, manageable tweaks that provide meaningful growth in different areas of the sales process.

As we go through the rest of this chapter on client acquisition, I'm going to share some strategies for how to increase all three areas we discussed here: conversion rate, average sale size, and prospect pipeline. But before you continue on, take a few minutes to think about how much you want to increase your revenues. Using the Sales C.A.P. Formula as your guide, write down the number by which you'd have to increase your sales conversion rate, average sale size, and prospect pipeline to get there.

Now we're going to get a bit more tactical. Here are some powerful strategies you can use to increase each of those three critical areas for sales growth.

SELL TO THE RIGHT CLIENTS

This sounds obvious, doesn't it? And yet many CEOs of organizations looking to increase sales struggle to answer the question, "Who is your ideal client?" When I sit down with these CEOs and ask that all-important question, I usually get a long-winded answer without a clear point. This is symptomatic of bigger, more dangerous problems that will ultimately hurt the company's top line.

You need to know exactly who your ideal client is. Otherwise, your sales team can't effectively sell to the right clients. Now, identifying your ideal client doesn't mean you'll never sell to someone who sits outside that ideal range. But by having a clear profile of your ideal client, you can focus your client acquisition strategy on going after those key opportunities. If you want to increase your close ratio and your average sale size, the best way to do that is to ensure that you're selling to the right clients.

If you want to increase your close ratio and your average sale size, the best way to do that is to ensure that you're selling to the right clients.

You can take steps right now to start targeting the right clients. Begin by segmenting your current client base into categories A, B, C, and D. Rank them based on the qualities described in the following chart:

A clients	B clients	C clients	D clients
Ideal clients you wish you had more of	The majority of your client list	You sell to these clients, but there's no love	They can't afford your offerings
Clients who buy your most premium and profitable offerings	They tend to buy middle-of-the-range offerings	They buy in small quantities, and beat you down on price	You try to avoid them
If you could have more of these clients, everything would change	You need a lot of B clients to equal the value of one A client	They require the most amount of service and can be frustrating clients	Not your ideal clients in any way

Once you've categorized your current clients, it's time to ask: Where do you focus your time? You should be spending 100% of your time on As and Bs. If you're spending time selling to Cs and Ds, you're wasting your salespeople's bandwidth, stretching the capacity of your customer service, and putting a strain on operations. In reality, these C and D clients aren't doing anything for your company.

While I'm not suggesting that you "fire" all of your C and D clients right away, you should make a clear policy moving forward: Sales efforts should only focus on the As and Bs from now on. I would suggest the following breakdown in terms of sales bandwidth:

- Spend 85% of time selling to As
- Spend 15% of time selling to Bs
- Spend 0% of time selling to Cs and Ds

Remember that just one A client is worth many Bs to your organization.

WHO ARE YOU GOING AFTER RIGHT NOW?

There's a good chance that you're not entirely clear about which clients your sales team is going after. You're not alone. But the truth is, senior management should be dictating explicitly who the sales team is selling to.

In sales, we have the popular concept of "Top 20 Prospects." This is often used on an individual level to help salespeople prioritize their prospecting activities by listing out the top 20 prospects they want to sell to. One of the most powerful strategies you can implement is to create a Top 20 Prospects list for your company. What are those 20 organizations that would make a massive dent in your sales, if you could get them as clients? Use this question to guide your creation of a Top 20 Prospects list for your organization. These should all be A clients, of course.

Senior management should be dictating explicitly who the sales team is selling to.

Once you have your list, a powerful exercise is to conduct meetings with both your sales team and your sales management team to lay out the top 20 accounts they should be going after. Be crystal clear about who these organizations are and gather as much information as possible about each account to help your sales team get laser-focused on those top 20 prospects.

Keep in mind that you may want to identify more than 20 top prospects for this exercise, particularly if you're selling a broader range of small products. In that case, create a list of top 40 or 50 prospects for your sales team to focus on. Even if your list is longer, your priority is still to become hyper-clear on who those organizations are, and which salespeople are expected to go after which accounts. This is going to be absolutely critical when we start to talk about accountability on your sales team.

CASE STUDY: CLIENT PRIORITIZATION

A client of mine that's a large manufacturer in the building product space sells mostly to very large national contractors. Upon initial review, we discovered that the salespeople weren't prioritizing the types of clients and prospects they were going after. They were pursuing small contractors with as much zeal and vigor as they pursued large contractors. Because of this simple prioritization error, sales were far below what they should have been.

To remedy this issue, we ranked the top 50 national contractors, some of whom were clients and some of whom were prospects. We categorized these contractors as As. We then ranked contractors 51 to 150 as Bs, and then everything below as Cs and Ds not to be pursued. By focusing the sales team's efforts only on As and Bs, salespeople's time suddenly freed up to spend more resources on those best targets.

As a result, within six months, the organization was able to close an additional $4 million in business from just a few large new sales. Some of the Cs and Ds continued to come through the door, but by prioritizing salespeople's time exclusively on As and Bs, the organization was able to grow sales without expending more resources to do so.

Remember: None of the organizations on your list should be C or D opportunities. The vast majority should be As, along with a few Bs that show high potential to turn into A clients down the road. Taking C and D prospects off the table is a critical strategic shift for most organizations, since selling to A opportunities is the single fastest way to increase sales. Although your A prospects will have a similar conversion rate to smaller, less ideal organizations, they'll also have a far larger transaction size.

> *Selling to A opportunities is the single fastest way to increase sales.*

If you were only going to implement one component of the Sales C.A.P. Formula (which, of course, you won't), increasing the average transaction size would give you the most amount of short-term change in the least amount of time. So, get your salespeople to focus more on those bigger fish.

YOUR CURRENT VALUE PROPOSITION

Of course, if you want your salespeople to start reeling in those bigger fish, you need to get crystal-clear on a value proposition that will compel A clients to buy from you, again and again. Let's take a look at your existing value proposition by doing a little exercise that will tell us everything we need to know:

1. Pull out a blank piece of paper and write for 30 seconds to answer this question: Why should a prospect work with your organization? Be sure to put this book down and write for 30 seconds straight. It should be just a sentence or two.

2. Next, imagine you've just been fired from your organization. If you're the owner of your company, imagine you've been kicked out. In the aftermath, you've been hired to run sales at one of your biggest competitor organizations. This is an organization that you've consistently gone to battle with in the past, from a sales perspective. You're now in charge of sales for that company.

3. With this mindset, pull out another piece of paper and write for 30 seconds to answer this question: Why should a prospect work with your (new) organization?

Chances are, you're looking at the blank page in front of you like a deer in headlights. I've done this exercise with thousands of CEOs over the years. In almost every instance, their answers to the two questions posed above are *exactly the same*. And that, my friend, is a huge problem.

When the answer to why people should do business with you is the same as why they should do business with your biggest competitor, you know you're in a lot of trouble. One thing I always talk about with salespeople is this: When you're perceived by prospects as being just like all other salespeople out there, you're dead in the water.

You can't afford to be just another option.

The same is true for businesses. In today's marketplace, there are simply too many options available to your prospects. You can't afford to be just another option. Instead, you must be uniquely situated from a selling perspective in the eyes of your prospective clients.

Take a look at what you wrote for your own company's value proposition. Most of the time, CEOs who write these statements focus on themselves, looking inward at their own company. But the proper focus of a value statement should be the prospect organizations you want to work with—not yourself.

When you say things like, "We have the best service, the highest quality products, the best people, the best customer service, and the longest track record in the industry," your prospects are rolling their eyes. These are all great features of any business, but in reality, every company touts those same exact benefits. It means nothing.

> *Prospects care about two things, and two things only: solving their challenges and accomplishing their key objectives.*

Just think of a competitive organization in your industry that has the absolute worst service you've ever seen. Do you think their salespeople are out there telling prospects, "Well, our service could use some work..." Of course they're not. They're still saying they have the best service around, even though it's not true. This is problematic for salespeople everywhere, because it means that prospects won't trust what they say—even in cases where it's true. Prospects have been burned too many times by organizations that talk relentlessly about how great they are, only to be disappointed by the actual product or service under the hood.

In light of all this, prospects certainly don't expect salespeople to focus exclusively on the prospect in their value proposition. So that's exactly what your sales team is going to do.

YOUR PROSPECT-CENTRIC VALUE PROPOSITION

The central question behind your new value proposition is: *What do your prospects care about?*

In general, prospects care about two things, and two things only: solving their challenges and accomplishing their key objectives. If your value proposition doesn't focus on either of these, then your salespeople are simply a time-suck in the eyes of the prospect. It's time to craft a value proposition that focuses on solving your prospects' key challenges and accomplishing key client objectives.

Let's begin:

1. Make a list of the top three objectives that your ideal clients are typically looking to accomplish.

2. Make a separate list of the top three to five challenges that your A clients are dealing with right now. Make sure these challenges fall within your company's domain. For example, if your organization is a marketing consultancy, then come up with three to five marketing challenges you solve. If you're a manufacturer, then think about the manufacturing challenges your best clients are dealing with. And so on.

3. Now that you have those two lists, it's time to circle the most common and critical objective shared by your ideal clients. This objective will be the anchor of your new value proposition.

4. Next, circle the most common and critical three challenges that your company can help clients solve.

5. Using your one objective and three challenges, fill in the blanks of the sentences below:

We help our clients [objective].

Typically, our clients come to us when they're dealing with [challenge 1], [challenge 2], or [challenge 3].

 You can download a free PDF version of this template in my Key Pages & Worksheets Guide at www.MarcWayshak.com/HighVelocity.

This might seem overly simplified, but the most powerful value propositions are succinct, straightforward, and purely focused on prospects' objectives and challenges.

> **REAL-LIFE EXAMPLES:**
>
> ABC Co. is an exhibition and event marketing support provider that empowers organizations to grow relationships between audiences and brands. Our clients come to us when they're: Worried about declining show attendance; struggling to get new or retain existing exhibitors; or, finally, they're just lacking show growth.
>
> XYZ Wealth Advisors helps clients make smart financial decisions. Clients typically come to us when they: Don't know if they're getting the right return on their money; are concerned about whether they're prepared for the next downturn; or, finally, they have a complex collection of random accounts in different places.

With your brand new value proposition as a starting point, take time to speak with other folks on your team—or even some of your best clients—to refine it. Feel free to change specific language or sentence structure, but be sure to use this simple template as the foundation for your new and improved value proposition.

Chapter 6:

Formal Sales Process

THIS IS NOT a sales training book. My goal is not to teach you how to sell. Chances are, you're in your current position today because you were very good at selling at some point in your career.

However, just because we ourselves are highly effective in selling situations doesn't mean other people at our organization can just flip a switch and do what we can do. One of the most common challenges faced by top-salespeople-turned-management is that they often don't understand exactly what makes them so effective at selling. When they try to teach others in the organization to do what they do, too much gets lost in translation.

To avoid this common pitfall, we're going to talk about how to implement a formal sales process. It's critical that every high-velocity sales organization has a consistent sales process that the entire sales team follows. This isn't just my opinion: Studies show that high-performing sales teams are 2.9 times more likely than under-performers to provide clients with a consistent experience.[53] Research also shows that best-in-class firms are 53% more likely than under-performing companies to invest in formal learning applications for their sellers.[54] This kind of structured selling approach leads to better training, development, and bottom-line results for sales teams across industries.

Without formalized consistency across the board, managing a sales team looks a lot like herding cats.

While the data clearly shows that organizations *should* make a consistent, long-term investment in providing salespeople with the basic tools to sell, this is rarely done well. Instead, many companies simply put the onus on sales managers or salespeople themselves to handle their own training, identify their own tools, and ultimately formulate their own sales strategy.

In the worst cases, this is an utter disaster. In the best cases, it leads to a complete lack of quality control. You might have one top performer who's doing a lot right, while the vast majority in the middle are providing a totally different experience to prospects. Without formalized consistency across the board, managing a sales team looks a lot like herding cats.

It's up to you, as the company leader, to change this reality. But like I said, this isn't a sales training book. So, in this chapter, we're going to focus on what you, as the company leader, need to know about the sales process—not everything your salespeople need to know.

KNOWLEDGE AND TRAINING

If your sales team doesn't have easy, direct access to sales training and sales knowledge at your organization, you'll never be able to implement a formal sales process. Simply put, knowledge and training form the foundation of any successful sales process. Without a clear way for your salespeople to access and benefit from the same resources across the board, selling consistency will remain impossible to achieve.

62% of HR managers admit they aren't doing a good job meeting learners' needs at their organization.

That's why the first step to building a strong foundation for your new sales process is to create a centralized sales knowledge bank where all your selling resources— from sales strategies to value proposition to effective proposals to marketing assets—are in one easily accessible place. This might sound obvious, but surprisingly few companies do this properly. In fact, 62% of HR managers admit they aren't doing a good job meeting learners' needs at their organization.[55]

While salespeople in the top 10% generally follow an organized, repeatable sales process, the rest tend to follow a more haphazard approach to selling.[56] It's no wonder why: When I first come into organizations to help them, the majority have their selling resources scattered in a wide range of confusing places. As a result, they hardly ever get utilized.

There's no excuse for this, since all it takes is a Google Doc, an X drive, or even a component of your existing CRM system to create a centralized place for all your sales knowledge. This is the first critical step to setting up a sales process that your sales team can actually follow easily, every day, without making it hard for them to implement.

In addition to the centralized database, your organization must have access to some type of sales training course that the whole team has gone through. Make sure it utilizes at least some online training. That way, each salesperson can finish the course at his or her own pace. It's up to management to make sure everyone completes it. After completing the online training, the entire sales team can go back to reference what they've learned at any time. But most important, every single member of the sales team must be required to complete the exact same sales training. This is critical to making sure the sales team is all speaking the same selling language.

With my own clients, I'm always sure to use a relatively even mix of live, face-to-face sales training combined with online reinforcement training.

YOUR NEW SALES PROCESS

Now, let's dive head-first into what you need to know in order to implement a successful sales process at your organization. Here are the three key areas of sales strategy we're going to focus on:

1. **Lead generation:** What strategies are the most effective at helping your salespeople get leads? The less labor-intensive the strategy, the more sustainable, and thus effective. Without effective lead generation, your salespeople are sitting ducks. They've got no leads to go after.

2. **Conversion:** What is the exact process by which your salespeople take leads and efficiently convert them into clients? Without the right conversion strategy, your salespeople are banging their heads against the wall, losing deal after deal, and they're not even sure why.

3. **Account management:** Once prospects become clients, how do your salespeople maintain them as clients, minimize attrition, and increase the amount the clients spend? Without an intentional account management strategy in place, your salespeople are like Sisyphus endlessly pushing the rock up the hill. They close new sales while losing existing clients out the back end.

These are the three areas where you can generate additional revenues at your company. To begin, let's focus on the nuts and bolts of effective lead generation.

LEAD GENERATION

First, let's get one thing straight: With very few exceptions, your salespeople are *not* 100% responsible for generating their own leads. In fact, as a rule of thumb, your organization should provide at least 25% of each salesperson's leads. This means that salespeople are responsible for 75% of their own lead generation, but the other 25% is up to your company— more specifically, your marketing team.

It's simply bad business to expect salespeople to generate all of their leads on their own.

Just to provide context, my data shows that 77.3% of companies today are providing at least 25% of a salesperson's total leads, with the most common split between lead sources being 25% inbound and 75% outbound.[57]

While you should focus on giving your salespeople the tools to generate as many of their own leads as possible, it's simply bad business to expect them to generate all of their leads on their own. Very few organizations have a marketing team strong enough to provide 100% of leads. In fact, only 9.3% of companies provide 100% of leads to the sales team.[58] Still, every marketing team should be able to provide at least some leads to the sales team. A solid goal is 25%.

At the end of the day, marketing's key role is to provide salespeople with leads. If marketing fails at this critical task, what is its purpose? It's crucial that everything your marketing team does is directly measurable.

This starts with changing the way you think about compensating the head of your marketing department. If your head of marketing is bonused on the amount of views, impressions, or clicks their material gets, you're focused on the wrong things. The only measurable factor that should matter to the head of marketing is the ability to provide the sales team with leads. Period.

WHY MARKETING IS SO IMPORTANT

In 2017, the Aberdeen Group released a study that showed 74% of best-in-class organizations have strong—or complete—alignment between marketing and sales.[59] I would go a step further and say that if you lack alignment between marketing and sales, not only will you never be best-in-class...you'll never even be *somewhat good.*

As an example of alignment between marketing and sales, a recent analysis of over 2,000 organizations found that sales teams who attempted to reach marketing leads within an hour were nearly seven times more likely to have meaningful conversations with decision makers than those who waited even 60 minutes.[60] Few companies have this seamless handoff between sales and marketing.

In a study that tested the response time of 433 companies, only 7% of sales teams responded in the first five minutes after a marketing form submission. More than half didn't respond within five business days,[61] proving that alignment between marketing and sales at a majority of organizations is missing.

> *74% of best-in-class organizations have strong—or complete—alignment between marketing and sales.*

At many organizations, this lack of alignment between sales and marketing is glaringly obvious, with the two departments being openly hostile to one another. This spells out the death of any organization, no matter how much it might excel in other areas. Why? Because marketing should be providing a healthy share of leads and assets that salespeople use to convert prospects into business. This is integral to the success of any company.

Take a look at the pyramid that follows, depicting the sales funnel from a marketing perspective:

As you can see, what matters most from a marketing standpoint is the actual number of leads provided to sales. This number is reflected at the bottom of the pyramid: sales qualified leads (SQLs), which are simply leads generated by marketing that sales says are acceptable quality leads. Your head of marketing should be focusing exclusively on SQLs. That's it. This is why every organization needs some reliable way to measure SQLs. Otherwise, you have no real way of knowing how effective your marketing department is.

What's more, when marketing lives and dies by SQLs, their incentives are aligned with sales. This mitigates tension between the two departments because when incentives are aligned, marketing is happy when sales is happy. Much of the common tension between marketing and sales comes down to a simple misalignment of incentives.

While 30% of sales teams rate marketing leads as poor quality, 49% of marketers believe the leads they send to sales are very high quality.

Another critical source of tension lies in the types of activities marketing chooses to spend time on. For various reasons, marketing teams often choose to focus time and effort on activities that don't directly benefit the sales team. What's more, sales and marketing tend to have vastly different opinions of what qualifies as a high-quality lead: While 30% of sales teams rate marketing leads as poor quality, 49% of marketers believe the leads they send to sales are very high quality.[62]

The following diagram helps to explain the dynamics at play:

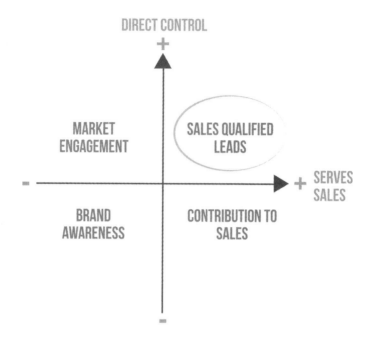

A lot of marketing folks spend their energy in the two left quadrants. This area includes efforts such as Facebook or other social media engagement. While a Facebook post might rack up thousands of likes, if it doesn't generate leads, it's a waste. Activities like this give marketing a lot of control, which is why they're popular. But as I said, they don't really serve sales.

Marketing has even less control over activities like publishing PR puff pieces that link back to the company website—and those efforts rarely serve sales, either. Still, it's a common time-suck for marketing folks, unless it's generating greater SEO, thus improving site ranking and leading to more inquiries.

So, you want your marketing team to exclusively focus on the two right quadrants above. While marketing folks don't have much control over their contribution to sales— that is, the amount of revenue generated from the leads marketing provides to sales—you can easily measure it with a good CRM system. SQLs, on the other hand, are both directly measurable and give marketing lots of direct control. That's why it's the sweet spot.

SELF-GENERATED LEADS

We've talked about how marketing can help provide those 25% of leads to your marketing team. Now we'll talk about the 75% that your salespeople are responsible for.

Before we begin, consider that over 40% of salespeople say prospecting is the most challenging part of their job.[63] My data shows that only 33% of salespeople have actually reached out to more than 250 prospects in the past year.[64]

This is why your lead generation assets are so important. Lead generation assets refer to the valuable resources available to your salespeople to help them generate qualified leads.

First, let's take stock of the lead generation assets you have right now: *What resources do you currently have that are valuable to prospects, and that actively help your salespeople get a foot in the door with prospective clients?*

Over 40% of salespeople say prospecting is the most challenging part of their job.

In today's world of selling, making old-school cold calls is rarely ever the most effective or efficient way to generate leads. Instead, you need to have valuable assets on hand that can help your salespeople generate their own leads in more creative, more personal, and smarter ways. A recent study by Thomas International found that the most important source of generated leads are what we call "self-generated leads,"[65] which are leads that come from salespeople themselves. Yet, 53.8% of sales-people report that it's harder or much harder to get in front of new prospects than it was five years ago.[66] So, what's the best way to produce more high-quality, self-generated leads at your organization?

The answer is simple: the sales prospecting campaign.

SALES PROSPECTING CAMPAIGN

This is where the sales prospecting campaign sweeps in to transform your sales process. The campaign is a fully mapped-out strategy for prospecting to prospective clients.

Think of the typical prospecting process: It's usually highly haphazard. It might involve identifying prospects and making a random number of calls, sending a few emails, and potentially mailing something. There's never a truly systematic process in place where salespeople can visually map out what they plan to do, when they plan to do it, and how to follow up.

The key to the sales prospecting campaign is that it enables salespeople to get on buyers' radar before they ever get them on the phone. Since only 19% of buyers actually want to connect with a salesperson during the initial awareness stage of their buying process,[67] it's important that salespeople are providing information to prospects early on in a systematic way, essentially warming up the relationship before the first point of contact.

The more you script out this process for salespeople, the more effective they'll be at prospecting. Don't leave it to your salespeople to develop their own prospecting process. It's on you to provide the framework for prospecting, and I'm going to lay it all out for you right here:

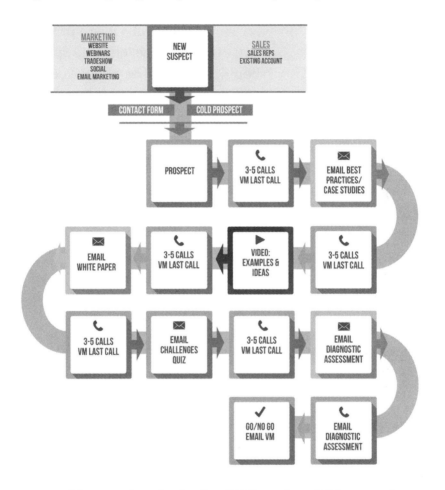

 You can download a free PDF version of this campaign chart in my Key Pages & Worksheets Guide at www.MarcWayshak.com/HighVelocity.

To implement a successful sales prospecting campaign, your sales leadership team needs to be fully invested. Work together with your sales leaders to map out the campaign your salespeople will use. Create a poster of the campaign flow that you can put on the walls at the office, where your salespeople can reference it whenever they need to.

The key to this strategy is that every single salesperson must follow it with every single prospect. Once a prospect is in the CRM system, salespeople should follow the flow of the campaign, and use carefully scripted templates for each phase of outreach. This is not an opportunity for improvisation. In fact, every high-velocity sales organization should create scripted phone call, email, and even LinkedIn message templates that can be used by salespeople with minimal customization for every prospect at each stage of the prospecting campaign.

Don't leave it to your salespeople to develop their own prospecting process.

Together, all of these different pieces keep your salespeople from just winging the lead generation process.

LEAD GENERATION ASSETS

Now, let's circle back around to your lead generation assets. As we discussed earlier in this chapter, these assets are the valuable resources available to your salespeople to help them generate qualified leads. They're also the backbone of your sales prospecting campaign. The success of all the calls, emails, LinkedIn messages, and voicemails in the campaign rely on the quality of the assets your salespeople have to offer their prospects.

I'm going to give you six examples of lead generation assets that my clients have used over the years—a sampling of the very best:

1. **Municipality Health Comparison Report:** One of my clients is a large organization that sells services to municipalities. They have access to a public database of available information on the municipalities they sell to, which allows them to easily put together reports for prospective clients that compare the health of their municipality to others in the same state. Using a number of different metrics from the publicly available data, my client creates a "Municipality Health Comparison Report" for salespeople to give out to prospects. Not only are these reports high-value, but they also help salespeople get a solid foot in the door by offering to put together a report for free.

2. **YouTube Channel Report:** A client of mine helps companies improve their YouTube channels. They target thought leaders or companies who have a strong YouTube following, but still have lots of room to expand. Before connecting with new prospects, my client does about 15 minutes of research on the prospect's YouTube channel. Using the data available, they provide a "YouTube Channel Report" for free in an email to provide valuable information up front to their prospects. It's such useful information that prospects think, "If they gave me this report for free, I wonder what kind of value I'd get if I worked with this company directly."

3. **Branding Assessment:** One of my clients is a promotional branding firm. They put together a "Branding Assessment" for prospects that shows the consistency of the organization's brand across such areas as digital presence, customer experience, and opportunities for improvement. These little reports give salespeople a

unique resource to offer in their first conversations with prospects. It's easy to do, and high value.

4. **Secret Shopping Report:** I worked with a company that sold consulting services to retailers, both online and brick-and-mortar. They used secret shopping as a powerful tool to create high-value reports for prospects. The salespeople went through the buying process at each prospective retailer, and then put together a report that noted strengths, weaknesses, and areas for improvement. By providing this "Secret Shopping Report" to prospects, salespeople were able to spark phone calls or even face-to-face meetings with top retailers.

5. **White Papers:** One client of mine, a leadership consulting firm, put together a huge cache of white papers that established them as experts in their space, positioning them as the authority on leadership development. These pre-written papers were used as valuable assets throughout the prospecting process, in the form of free giveaways to prospects.

6. **FedEx Mail:** Never underestimate the value of actually mailing something to a prospect. Mail is a powerful asset, and one of the easiest ways to stand out from the competition. In today's email-driven world, organizations focus much of their energy on emailing assets to prospects. This opens up a tremendous opportunity for savvy companies to mail packages to prospects instead.

I'm not suggesting that your salespeople send just any old brochure in the mail. The key is to send something valuable, useful, and relevant to the prospect. Once they have that, your salespeople should mail it using FedEx. Word to the wise: Everyone opens a FedEx package—even the CEO. Couple that with a hand-addressed envelope, and your sales team will dramatically increase the likelihood of high-value prospects opening their packages.

Now, look back at this sales prospecting campaign example:

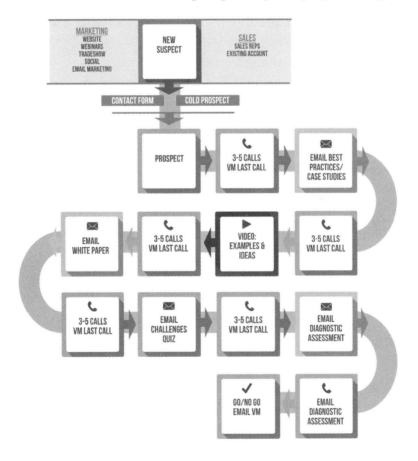

Hopefully, it's clear how these lead generation assets fit within the sales prospecting campaign. The key is that every single attempt at contact has an explicit purpose. Salespeople are never just calling prospects to "check in" or "pick their brain"—instead, there's a specific reason behind every point of outreach. These repeated attempts at contact are the hallmark of the sales prospecting campaign. They ultimately serve two functions:

1. Throughout the campaign, the prospect becomes increasingly more familiar with the salesperson. By the time the salesperson gets the prospect on the phone, the prospect knows exactly who the salesperson is.

2. Salespeople will never have to make a true cold call again.

The most successful campaigns make about 20 "touches" to each prospect. The data shows that it takes an average of 18 calls to actually connect with a buyer, and only 24% of sales emails are actually opened.[68] Remember, each touch includes something like a mailed asset, a round of phone calls, an email, a LinkedIn message, etc. Thanks to the tools included in most CRM systems today, salespeople can automate a good amount of this process. A strong CRM system can enable your sales team to map out the entire process so all they have to do is follow the prompts for each step. The system will automatically move them along. This is a key part of the process I regularly help clients set up.

In the end, this sales prospecting campaign is the most effective way for your salespeople to get in front of prospects they have no direct connection to, making it the best way for them to produce self-generated leads.

HOSTING EXCLUSIVE EVENTS

If the sales prospecting campaign is the most important part of lead generation for your sales team, then hosting exclusive events is your most critical lead generation task as a company leader. This is the one lead generation opportunity that can really be driven by management. Exclusive events are one of the most effective tools an organization can implement to support salespeople in their effort to get in front of high-level prospects.

Hosting exclusive events means hosting live, in-person events multiple times a year. Your sales and management teams should invite all their top clients and prospects to attend. At each event, plan to share valuable information with attendees. This shouldn't be a sales pitch, but rather an opportunity for attendees to network with other like-minded executives and gain valuable knowledge to use in their day-to-day jobs.

Most important, it must feel like a truly exclusive event. I suggest you don't charge people to attend the event, but rather make it clear to those you invite that the event is exclusively for high-level individuals, such as CEOs, VPs, directors, and other senior leaders at your target organizations. Your best bet is to host the event at a venue that comes off as exclusive, such as a university club, a Ritz-Carlton, or some other high-end hotel chain with a recognizable brand.

On a personal note, this strategy totally transformed my business when I started hosting invitation-only events years ago. I typically host two of these events per year at a Harvard Club, and I only invite CEOs, presidents, and VPs of sales at companies that fit my target size.

Remember to have your sales team invite both A clients and prospects to this event. Encourage your salespeople to leverage their relationships to ask for introductions to other people who might want to attend. My clients typically get 20 RSVPs from direct invitations, but by simply asking those 20 RSVPs for introductions to other people, they can double that number. Ask everyone in your network for introductions to people who might want to come. It's the easiest introduction you can possibly ask for, because everyone wants to attend an exclusive event.

It's the easiest introduction you can possibly ask for, because everyone wants to attend an exclusive event.

On the day of the event, a senior leader of your organization should speak, sharing some industry best practices with the audience. You might also invite a guest speaker who is influential in the industry to address the crowd. Just having all of these people together provides huge value to those in the room. At the event, your top salespeople should be mingling and engaging with the prospects they invited. It's a gift to your salespeople to be able to interact with high-level prospects in such a setting. The goal should be to set up as many meetings as possible after the event.

This one strategy has directly led to hundreds of millions of dollars in business for my clients over the past few years. It's time for you to join them.

CONVERSION

Up until this point, we've focused on the area of client acquisition strategy that actually puts opportunities into the pipeline—opportunities that will feed leads to your sales team. While this area is undoubtedly critical, it's still just one part of a successful client acquisition. Now, I want to focus on the next piece of the puzzle: Once you actually have a warm body who's shown interest to the sales team, what are your salespeople doing to convert that prospect into a paying client?

In many cases, conversion is the most difficult area to tweak for organizations. It requires a consistent level of discipline, not only to introduce a solid strategy for conversion to the sales team, but also to reinforce that new strategy and ensure people are following through.

But the reality is, there are real strategies you can put in place at your organization to help your sales team effectively convert prospects into clients. Your new conversion process will have the power to dramatically shift the numbers in favor of your sales team, when it comes to how many prospects actually end up signing on the dotted line.

In my work with thousands of salespeople over the years, I've found that some salespeople are able to immediately grasp the conversion process, while others never quite seem to get it. What I can promise you is this: It will be abundantly clear who falls into which category, right away.

Your new conversion process will have the power to dramatically shift the numbers in favor of your sales team.

Your top performers are likely to "get" the conversion process immediately, while those salespeople who tend to fall in the bottom of your rankings will push back on these ideas with everything they have. I've seen it play out like this, time and time again, at a wide range of companies over the years.

Before we get into the details of what your conversion process should look like, let's see how your current conversion rate compares to that of other folks within your industry. My good friends over at HubSpot put together a powerful chart to help you do this, drawing data from their proprietary CRM platform tool to assess typical conversion rates based on industry. As you can see below, different industries have different levels of average conversion rates:

Sales Close Rate by Industry

arts & Entertainment	28%	Management Consulting	20%
Business & Industrial	27%	Finance	19%
Internet & Telecom	26%	Human Resources	18%
Autos & Vehicles	26%	Media	18%
Legal & Government	25%	Beauty & Fitness	17%
Computers & Electronics	23%	Healthcare	17%
Computer Software	22%	Non-Profit	17%
Construction	22%	Real Estate	17%
Design & Development	22%	Travel	16%
Public Relations and Communications	22%	Biotechnology	15%
Shopping	22%	Insurance	14%
Information Technology and Services	21%	Event Services	13%
Professional Training & Coaching	21%	Hospitality	11%
Agriculture	20%	Marketing and Advertising	11%
Jobs & Education	20%		

HubSpot

HubSpot is a sales and marketing software company with over 21,000 customers in more than 90 countries. HubSpot looked at over 8900 companies and 28 industries to calculate the average sales close rate (sales closed divided by total deals worked).

According to the graph, how does your organization compare to others in your industry? I'm willing to bet that many readers are looking at this chart unsure, because they're simply not tracking their conversion rate…so they don't even know what it is. If this sounds like you, you're far from alone.

Let's take a few minutes to figure out a ballpark estimate for your current conversion rate:

Total Number of Closed Sales

÷

Total Number of Leads or Opportunities

=

Your Current Conversion Rate

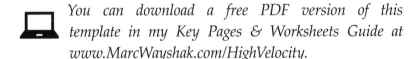 *You can download a free PDF version of this template in my Key Pages & Worksheets Guide at www.MarcWayshak.com/HighVelocity.*

Write down your number and try not to be demotivated if it seems low. Don't celebrate if it's too high, either. This could mean your people are cheating, and not putting early-stage opportunities in. Organizations without a clear, well thought-out sales process are likely to have conversion rates that are significantly lower than the average in their industry.

THE SALES CONVERSION PROCESS

Now that you have an idea of where you currently stand when it comes to conversion rate, let's talk about the concept of sales conversion in high-level terms. I want you to imagine you're in the process of manufacturing a product. You're starting out with some type of raw material, and eventually turning that material into a sellable, usable product. This process includes a regimented series of steps to turn the raw material into the end-product, and it's the same procedure every single time.

The sales conversion process is similar in many ways to this simple concept of manufacturing a product. You start with your raw material—a brand new prospect who has shown some type of interest in your company, whether via a cold call, a sales prospecting campaign, an internet contact form, or an introduction from an existing client. Then, the conversion process takes your raw material and turns it into your desired end-product: a paying client.

Much like a manufacturing process, a conversion process should be absolutely systematic. While you can't program a machine to do the job of sales conversion (yet), you *can* train your salespeople to think systematically about this process.

Here's why this is so important: At many organizations, salespeople are just winging the conversion process. There's no system at all. Those companies just expect salespeople to have their own personal plan for converting prospects into clients. As a result, many salespeople are highly transactional in their selling behaviors. They view their job as selling products or services, as opposed to engaging in consultative conversations with prospects to understand what they're looking for and determine the strength of the opportunity. It's not surprising, then, that buyers rate two-thirds of B2B salespeople as being average or poor.[69]

Without a clearly laid-out process, your salespeople will not only be clueless about how the sales process is progressing with each prospect, but they'll also lose out on many good opportunities. (The average sale size will also be much smaller than it otherwise could be—which, as you'll remember, is a key component of the Sales C.A.P. Formula we discussed in Chapter 5.)

> *Much like a manufacturing process, a conversion process should be absolutely systematic.*

What's required is a total mindset-shift. Your sales managers and salespeople need to start thinking about the sales conversion process as a systematic, replicable series of steps to convert prospects into clients. The best way to accomplish this is to present the conversion process as a simple system that your salespeople can easily articulate and visualize.

First things first, you must have a visual representation of your sales conversion process posted throughout the workplace, so that salespeople can constantly see it. That way, it's being reinforced when they're at their desks, at sales meetings, or just hanging out around the water cooler. For many of my clients, I customize this process from beginning to end. But I also have a more standard sales conversion process that you can implement at your own organization.

What follows is a visual of my standard conversion process:

 You can download a free PDF version of this process visual in my Key Pages & Worksheets Guide at www.MarcWayshak.com/HighVelocity.

ENGAGEMENT

I've said it before, and I'll say it again: This is not a sales training book. I'm simply focusing on what company executives absolutely must know in order to make sure their salespeople are effective at selling. Period. (If you're looking for a sales training book, I encourage you to grab a copy of my earlier book, *Game Plan Selling*.) That said, it's imperative that you stick with me here, because I'm going to walk you through—high-level—exactly what your sales team should be doing to maximize their sales conversions.

It all starts with a simple goal. Whenever I ask salespeople, "What's the goal of your first interaction with a prospect?" I get a wide range of answers: trying to make a sale, trying to create interest, trying to identify need. While none of these answers are inherently wrong, none are quite right, either.

> *The simple goal of any salesperson's first conversation with a prospect should be to create engagement.*

The simple goal of any salesperson's first conversation with a prospect should be to create engagement. That's it.

The very first part of a successful conversion process is just about engaging the prospect in a conversation. It's not about educating the prospect. It's not about showing the prospect how great the product is or persuading the prospect to buy. It's just about engaging the prospect in a conversation.

This incredibly simple idea in sales strategy is actually monumental. Many salespeople go into an initial prospect conversation ready to lay everything out on the table: all the benefits of the product they sell, all the reasons why the prospect should buy from them. But this couldn't be further from the right approach.

Just think about your own buying experiences. As a company leader, you're probably in buying positions pretty frequently. And when you are, do you enjoy conversations with high-pressure salespeople who are trying to sell you on something from the get-go? Of course you don't. The data shows that the three top reasons why buyers don't want to talk to salespeople are that 1) they feel pressure to buy, 2) they perceive salespeople as only caring about themselves, and 3) they're uncomfortable saying "no" to salespeople.[70]

Your salespeople need to flip the script of their initial conversations completely. Instead of focusing on themselves, they need to focus exclusively on engaging the prospect by talking about the challenges and objectives that affect the prospect most. The data couldn't be clearer on this. A recent Salesforce study showed that more than three-quarters (76%) of consumers say it's absolutely critical or very important to work with a salesperson who focuses on achieving client needs instead of making a quick sale.[71]

Focusing on client needs is also a major factor in whether prospects choose to work with you. In a comprehensive study by DemandBase, 64% of respondents said it was "very important" that the vendor they chose "demonstrated a stronger knowledge of our company and its needs" than competing vendors. Another 30% of respondents said it was "somewhat important"—and overall, it was the second most influential reason why buyers chose the winning vendor.[72]

OPENING PLAY

The single best way to start this type of sales conversation is with something I like to call the Opening Play. You've heard the terms "30-second commercial" or "elevator pitch" before—that's not what I'm talking about here. Instead of a cheesy, "me"-focused, fake-sounding pitch, the Opening Play is like a powerful kick-off in a football game. Its only purpose is to engage prospects in an interesting conversation *about them*.

Chances are, your salespeople have never mapped out the initial phase of engaging a prospect before. But the first part of a conversation with a stranger is the most important. In those first few seconds, we decide whether or not to continue the conversation—or end it immediately. That's why it's so important to implement a systematic, planned-out process for starting conversations with prospects.

Below is an example of what an Opening Play should sound like. You'll notice that it draws directly from the value proposition you created back in Chapter 5:

Opening Play

My company is a [your type of company]

that works with [type of clients you have]

to help our clients [very briefly describe what you do]

Typically, our clients come to us when they're dealing with:

[challenge #1]

[challenge #2]

[challenge #3]

Do any of those issues ring true to you?

 You can download a free PDF version of this template in my Key Pages & Worksheets Guide at www.MarcWayshak.com/HighVelocity.

The data shows that the more time salespeople spend on the phone talking about their company, the less likely they are to take the prospect to a next step.[73]

It's important to remember that there's no magic bullet to capturing prospects' attention and keeping it. But by using the first few seconds of the conversation to mention common challenges that organizations face in their world, your salespeople can vastly increase their chances of engaging prospects. Prospects will usually guide the salesperson to talk more about the one challenge that's most relevant—and critical—to them at the moment. It's a simple yet effective way to engage prospects in conversations that lead to high-value interactions, rather than surface-level exchanges about the benefits of a product or service. The more salespeople can get prospects to generate long responses, the more likely they are to close the sale.[74]

A shocking 77% of buyers believe that salespeople don't understand their problems enough to be able to help solve them.

Even so, I'll tell you right now that most of your salespeople will struggle to write their own Opening Play. The reason is that they've been thinking in terms of features and benefits up until this point. But prospects simply don't care about features and benefits, and it's imperative that your salespeople change their approach to reflect this undeniable reality. Prospects only care about the challenges that salespeople can solve for them. And yet, a shocking 77% of buyers believe that salespeople don't understand their problems enough to be able to help solve them.[75] The Opening Play addresses this directly, and that's why it's so powerful.

When having your salespeople create Opening Plays, it's important to note that not all Opening Plays will be appropriate for all prospects. The owner of an SME will require a different Opening Play than the marketing manager at a Fortune 500 company. Those two prospects face vastly different challenges. Every Opening Play must be adjusted accordingly.

My recommendation for introducing the Opening Play into your sales strategy is to meet with your sales team to come up with a list of key challenges that your organization solves for clients. Make sure these are true challenges, and not just the benefits your company provides to clients.

To adopt this technique fully as a sales organization, it's important that your salespeople agree on what those challenges are. As a group, come up with a generalized Opening Play that will work for most of your ideal prospects. Have your salespeople start to implement it right away. Remember, they can tweak this Opening Play, as needed, to fit the needs of specific clients as they come along.

A staggering 75% of initial sales calls fail to generate a second meeting simply because salespeople didn't know enough about the buyer's situation.

As your salespeople begin using the Opening Play, it's crucial that they really "get" the challenges they're talking about to prospects in those initial conversations. What I mean by that is, your salespeople need to know what it's like to be a user of the product or service they sell. Only then can they truly understand how clients' challenges are solved by it.

When salespeople don't fully understand their clients' circumstances, the sales cycle doesn't progress. In fact, a recent study found that a staggering 75% of initial sales calls fail to generate a second meeting simply because salespeople didn't know enough about the buyer's situation to provide the value needed to warrant the advancement of the sale.[76]

This piece is often missing from the sales training process altogether. Organizations are in such a rush to get their salespeople up and selling that they overlook this critical component of effective sales. It's nearly impossible for salespeople to sell consultatively when they don't understand firsthand the challenges being solved by the product or service. The best remedy is to require that your salespeople actually use the product or service they sell.

As part of your training initiative on the Opening Play, invite your salespeople to experience what your company offers. Follow the example of companies like HubSpot, which includes this concept as part of its innovative onboarding process for new sales recruits. Since HubSpot is a platform that helps small businesses create an online presence, new sales hires create a website using HubSpot's platform. They write blogs, build an online presence, and become full-fledged users of the platform. As a result, when they start selling, they can relate to the specific challenges that can be solved by HubSpot. It's no longer academic, but instead something they understand at their core, as users themselves.

It's nearly impossible for salespeople to sell consultatively when they don't understand firsthand the challenges being solved by the product or service.

I'll give you a couple of other great examples. One of my clients is a manufacturing company that has its salespeople spend a few days on-site with a key client. The goal is simple: Observe and participate in a day in the life of an ideal client. Salespeople help out on the floor, take direct orders from company leaders, and fill whatever role they can to get a sense of the work environment. This unique approach gives salespeople the opportunity to not only experience client challenges firsthand, but also to gain deeper perspective on the day-to-day operations of their target client.

Another client of mine sells seats to large live events such as concerts, theater shows, and festivals. Their new salespeople must attend one of these live events as a participant—tough gig, I know. This way, all of their salespeople are fully aware of the process of attending the events they sell tickets to. In addition, they gain a first-person perspective on the end-to-end experience of those events, making them more equipped to connect genuinely with prospects.

This will come easily to your best salespeople, who most likely already put themselves in the shoes of their clients when they sell. After all, one of the primary characteristics of top performers is their ability to see things from their clients' point of view.[77]

It's all part of a larger shift toward understanding what's going on inside the minds of prospects. *What do your prospects care most about? What do they want to accomplish? What do they struggle with?* The next piece to this puzzle will provide you and your sales organization with a clear framework for answering these critical questions.

DISQUALIFICATION CUPBAN

Disqualification is a sales strategy that's counter-intuitive for many sales leaders. In all likelihood, you were taught to qualify prospects during the sales process—or more traditionally, to persuade prospects to do business with you. Both of these ideas are antiquated.

Let's start with persuasion. Most salespeople today still try to persuade prospects to do business with them. There are more sales books out there on persuasion than on any other topic. But in reality, there's evidence that shows persuasive selling has the opposite of its intended effect. Due to the psychological concept of reactance, when a salesperson is trying to persuade a buyer, there is often a natural resistance to that persuasion. As a result, the buyer actually strengthens a view that's directly contrary to what the salesperson is saying.[78]

In reality, at least 50% of the opportunities your salespeople come across will not be a fit for your product or service.

The other problem with persuasion is insurmountable: When salespeople try to persuade prospects to do business with them, they're making assumptions about the prospects that are inherently flawed. They're assuming things about prospects that they can't possibly know. The biggest of these flawed assumptions is that every prospect is a fit for what the salesperson is selling.

In reality, at least 50% of the opportunities your salespeople come across will not be a fit for your product or service.[79] This is borne out as true in the conversion rates graph we looked at earlier in this chapter. Did you notice how even the highest conversion rates are only in the high 20-percent range? There's nothing to be afraid of when it comes to disqualifying at least half of the opportunities that your salespeople come across. In fact, a rate of disqualification like that would put your organization among the best of the best.

The top organizations in sales have mastered the system of disqualifying "bad fits" early on in the sales cycle. That's why I'm focusing so much on the topic of disqualification, and not at all on the idea of qualifying prospects. The point isn't to turn unqualified prospects into qualified ones. Instead, the goal is to disqualify those bad fits early on in the sales process.

The sooner your salespeople are disqualifying those poor opportunities, the sooner they will close the good opportunities. In sales, the scarcest resource of all is time—and sales reps today already only spend 36% of their time selling.[80] If your salespeople spend their time trying to convert prospects who aren't a good fit, they're wasting their number one resource.

> *Sales reps today already only spend 36% of their time selling.*

So, it's time to change the way your salespeople think about their opportunities. It's time to take them through this process of disqualifying those opportunities that aren't a good fit. This mindset change can best be described as shifting from thinking like salespeople to thinking like doctors.

I always use the example of when I went to a well-known, well-respected doctor in Boston to take care of an old rugby injury. I had torn the meniscus in my knee and lived with it for years until I finally made an appointment with this orthopedic surgeon.

"I'm pretty sure I need surgery," I told the doctor when I arrived. "What can you do for me?"

Now, the doctor didn't flash me a wide smile, enthusiastically shake my hand, and say, "Well, Marc, you've come to the right place! I know exactly how to fix you up in no time at all. I'll have you up and running in six weeks. Just sign on the dotted line and we'll get started!"

If he had done that, I would have run the other way—or, hobbled the other way. Instead, this thoughtful doctor took his time to examine my knee. He ran tests and scans. He watched me walk and took copious notes. And above all, he asked me questions—tons of questions—about my lifestyle, my current exercise regimen, my pain level, my plans for the future, and the challenges I'd faced because of my injury.

The top three ways to create a positive sales experience for buyers are 1) to listen to their needs, 2) don't be pushy, and 3) provide relevant information based on their needs.

At the end of this extensive process, the doctor finally recommended arthroscopic surgery. I trusted his recommendation and went ahead with the surgery because I could see his process for what it was: expert, genuine, thorough, and professional.

Of course, your salespeople aren't doctors performing surgery on prospects. But the lesson still couldn't be clearer. The vast majority of salespeople today are those quack doctors who flash a toothy grin before rushing to perform the most expensive, needless surgery, leaving the patient feeling taken advantage of, lost, and frustrated.

When your salespeople try to persuade prospects to buy from them, right off the bat, they don't just lose some credibility with potential clients. They completely *kill trust* at the very start of the sales process.

It's no surprise that the top three ways to create a positive sales experience for buyers are 1) to listen to their needs, 2) don't be pushy, and 3) provide relevant information based on their needs.[81] Only when your salespeople start thinking like good doctors will they make their prospects feel the way I felt with that orthopedic surgeon: in good hands.

I chose that doctor based on the level of comfort I felt with him. Remember, I have no ability to discern a particular doctor's technical expertise. I trusted him and felt confident that he could get me the results I wanted. Why? Because he took the time to understand my challenges completely.

Research shows that top-performing salespeople have the ability to see things from their clients' point of view.[82] In fact, a recent survey I conducted found that top performers are 30% more likely to report that their buyers think of them as experts in their field.[83] This is exactly what the Disqualification CUPBAN will enable your salespeople to do.

Now, I'm going to briefly walk you through the CUPBAN. The CUPBAN is circular because there's never a start or an end; rather, it's a constantly revolving process of six steps that repeat forever. Your sales CRM should reflect each of these six steps when you implement the CUPBAN into your sales strategy.

The following process visual lays out exactly what your salespeople should be doing to ensure they're disqualifying bad fits—and thus qualifying good opportunities:

1. Challenges

The first step of CUPBAN is all about digging deeper into prospects' challenges. As we've established many times in this book already, your salespeople must understand the challenges their prospects are facing. The Opening Play is the beginning of this process, a powerful launching pad for discovering what those challenges are. But after the Opening Play, your salespeople need to dig deeper to learn *more* about the prospect's top three most relevant challenges.

Here's the reasoning behind this first step in the CUPBAN process: Every single one of your salespeople should have a *thorough understanding* of the top three challenges their prospects are facing with regards to the product or service. This means that just knowing *what* the challenges are isn't enough. It needs to go deeper than that. Research shows that diving into three or four client problems correlates with the highest

> *Your salespeople must understand the challenges their prospects are facing.*

likelihood of advancing a deal to a solid next step.[84]

For example, if you're a company that offers a marketing service, your salespeople need to *thoroughly understand* the top three marketing challenges faced by prospects on a daily basis. Who do these challenges affect? Where do these challenges occur? Why are these challenges happening today?

If you're a company that manufactures building products, then your salespeople need to *thoroughly understand* the top challenges prospects are facing with regards to using products like yours. If you're an operational consulting firm, your salespeople/consultants need to *thoroughly understand* the top challenges prospects are facing within the domain of operations that your organization specializes in. And so on and so on.

Here are some questions your salespeople can ask to discover as much as they can about the prospect's top three challenges, directly following the Opening Play:

"Tell me more about your challenges with regards to _____."

"Can you give me some more insight into that?"

"Can you give me an example?"

2. Upside

This is probably the most overlooked, underrated component of the sales process. A whopping 79% of buyers say it's absolutely critical or very important for them to interact with a salesperson who is a trusted advisor who adds value to their business.[85]

Whether or not salespeople understand the upside of solving prospects' challenges is the key difference between prospects being willing to invest a lot of money in an offering, and prospects saying, "I don't have a budget for this." Upside is the heart of creating value in sales: "What would it mean to the prospect, in dollars, if their challenges could be solved?"

Here's a play-by-play of what an upside conversation sounds like:

AN UPSIDE CONVERSATION

Marketing salesperson: "What's the biggest marketing challenge your organization is facing right now?"

Prospect: "Well, we don't have good branding. Nobody even knows who we are."

Salesperson: "If you were able to solve this challenge so you were better known in the marketplace, what would it mean in potential upside to your organization?"

Prospect: "That would be huge. The upside would be enormous."

Salesperson: "I see. But in specific dollars, what could it mean in additional revenues to your organization?"

Prospect: "Well, it could mean at least an additional $10 million in revenues for us."

Time out. Go back and re-read the last sentence of that conversation. The prospect just said that solving the challenge of having weak brand recognition is worth *at least $10 million.*

Obviously that's not a direct line to what the prospect is willing to invest in a solution—but a line, no matter how thin, has still been drawn between the figure *$10 million* and *the value of a potential solution* to solve the challenge at hand. This is now the central value of what the salesperson is offering. If the product or service works, it's worth $10 million to the prospect, plain and simple.

When salespeople spend their time trying to show prospects that they're giving discounted pricing instead of creating value in the sale,

Top-performing reps spend 52% more time talking about value than average performers.

they're doing real damage to their chances of closing the deal. Research shows that when salespeople use the word "discount" during the sales process, it actually decreases close rates by 17%.[86]

That's why this upside piece is crucial for your salespeople to grasp. One of the top reasons buyers don't make a purchase is that salespeople can't fully articulate the value of using their product or service.[87] What's more, top-performing reps spend 52% more time talking about value than average performers.[88]

Especially in the B2B space, it's paramount that salespeople get an actual dollar amount tied to the upside of a potential solution to the prospect's challenge. The main question to implement in the sales process is this:

"If you could solve this challenge, what would be the upside, in dollars, to your organization?"

3. Personal

This third step of the disqualification process is one of the most controversial. The majority of salespeople are incredibly uncomfortable with making sales personal. In particular, most salespeople in the B2B space avoid having conversations about personal objectives altogether. But the reality is that, thanks to brain imaging technologies, we now know that all decisions are driven first and foremost by emotions.[89] This means that prospects will only choose to make an investment if there is a *personal benefit* to making that investment.

Thanks to brain imaging technologies, we now know that all decisions are driven first and foremost by emotions.

This is true across the board, and even in the B2B space. If there's no personal benefit to solving a challenge, then prospects simply won't invest in a solution. Period. Salespeople need to think more deeply—like psychologists—to understand the real intentions behind the decisions prospects make.

As my mentor Alan Weiss once told me, "Behind every business objective is a personal objective." It's up to your salespeople to discover the personal objectives held by each and every prospect they connect with. By understanding the personal motivations behind solving business challenges, salespeople will get a much clearer sense of how driven prospects are to actually buy. Not all business objectives are created equal, and not all business challenges are equally critical to solve. The most important are those that have the strongest personal effect on the prospect.

One of my clients sells services to the federal government. When speaking with a government bureaucrat who is in charge of the decision-making process, my client needs to understand how solving the challenge will affect that bureaucrat *personally*. If the bureaucrat doesn't feel personal skin in the game, it won't happen. The prospect needs to be feeling direct accountability or pressure of a personal nature in order to close the deal.

Here are the most effective questions your salespeople can ask at this point in the CUPBAN process:

"How does this challenge affect you personally?"
"What would it mean to you personally if this challenge were solved?"

4. <u>Budget</u>

Your salespeople absolutely must talk about money before they start to present their solution to prospects. Why? Almost half of all deals are lost because of budget.[90] My own research shows that budget is the number one reason that strong opportunities fall apart: 55% of salespeople list budget as the first or second most common reason for opportunities falling apart.[91]

The traditional model of selling has salespeople present their solution, along with pricing, up front to anyone who will listen. This approach not only gives away massive amounts of valuable information for free—essentially unpaid consulting—but also shoots salespeople in the foot by having them put out a price before they fully understand the ins and outs of the opportunity.

If your salespeople simply throw out a price before having the "money conversation" with prospects, there will be one of two consequences: either they'll blow the prospect out of the water by coming in too high, or they'll come in way under what the prospect had imagined, leaving a lot of money on the table—and possibly scaring the prospect off because it sounds too cheap.

Budget is the number one reason that strong opportunities fall apart in sales.

Understanding budget before giving price is also a key indicator of prospects' seriousness in making an investment. For example, if your organization's typical offering is $100,000, but the prospect's budget caps out at just $25,000, then that prospect is immediately disqualified. Your salespeople shouldn't spend time and effort on those prospects who could never afford to buy in the first place.

The key here is to ask a simple, two-part budget question. Here's the first part:

"What could you see investing to fix these problems?"

Often, prospects will answer this question vaguely, saying, "I'm not sure...I haven't thought about a specific number...I still need to figure that out..."

If this happens, it's time for the second part of the question, which I call The Range Question:

"I totally understand. To avoid the back and forth about budget, I can tell you that typically the investment required for what we're talking about would be somewhere between $___ and $___. Where could you see yourself on that spectrum?"

It's important that the first dollar amount is on the lower end of budget, while the second is on the very high end. There should be a really big spread between the two numbers, such as $50,000 and $250,000, or $10,000 and $100,000, or even $2 million and $6 million. Yes, these are

On average, 6.8 people are involved in every business purchasing decision.

massive ranges, but this is intentional. Your salespeople need to use numbers that give prospects enough range to feel comfortable putting themselves somewhere on the spectrum. Suddenly, they'll have a budget. When you look at pipeline reports, you should see these budget conversations recorded by your salespeople. Otherwise, they're leaving money on the table.

5. <u>A</u>uthority

This step is all about decision making. At this point in the sales process, your salespeople need to determine the answers to the following questions: Is the prospect a decision maker? Who else is involved? What does the decision-making process look like? How long does it take?

Many salespeople stop when they have the answer to the first question—*Is the prospect a decision maker?* But in reality, this is just the tip of the iceberg.

Knowing whether the prospect is a decision maker is useless if the decision-making process still involves going to the board or getting buy-in from other decision makers at the company. While 64% of the C-suite has final sign-off on buying decisions, a whopping 81% of employees not in the C-suite influence purchasing decisions.[92] And, on average, 6.8 people are involved in every business purchasing decision.[93] Knowing what the decision-making process looks like, from end to end, is a key part of understanding how qualified an opportunity truly is.

It's also something that prospects appreciate. A study published in the *Harvard Business Review* showed that buyers' most common grievance against salespeople was that they didn't follow the structured purchasing process in place at the buyers' companies.[94]

The question your salespeople should ask is simple:

"What is your typical decision-making process for a project like this?"

The prospect should explain what that process looks like, in detail, before the salesperson moves on.

6. <u>N</u>ext step

One of the most common mistakes salespeople make is neglecting to set a clear, scheduled next step. Setting scheduled next steps is one of the strongest indicators of sales velocity. Salespeople who live by setting clear, scheduled next steps have a much higher pipeline velocity than those who don't. I can't tell you the number of times

Successful sales involve 12.7% more time devoted to discussing next steps than unsuccessful sales.

I've sat in on pipeline meetings and asked, "What are the next steps on this opportunity?" only to get the following response: "Oh, I'm just supposed to check in with the prospect in a month." This is the kiss of death. Unclear, weak, unscheduled, nothing.

A clear, scheduled next step means that a calendar invite went out and was accepted by the prospect. It could be an invitation for a call in two months, but it absolutely must be scheduled. Otherwise, it doesn't really exist. Within the context of this CUPBAN process, a next step could also mean putting together a proposal or giving a presentation.

At the end of every meeting, your salespeople should be creating a next step. If this is the only thing your salespeople learn, they'll still increase their sales. Data recently collected by the AI conversion platform Gong.io shows that successful sales involve 12.7% more time devoted to discussing next steps than unsuccessful sales.[95]

To start the process of scheduling a next step, your salespeople can ask:

"Do you have your calendar open right now?"

As you can see, the CUPBAN process is very simple. That's what makes it so effective. Hopefully, you're starting to see how this can translate directly into your team's CRM opportunities. As a sales leader in your organization, you should be able to access this information for every single opportunity that comes through.

Your salespeople should never give a prospect a proposal until they thoroughly understand what's going on in the prospect's world.

In the infrastructure section of this book, we'll talk specifically about how you can do that. But for now, suffice to say that your sales team's CRM should contain fields for each opportunity that show these six CUPBAN steps, so you can easily refer to and track them.

PROPOSALS

At this point you're probably thinking to yourself, "Marc keeps saying this isn't a sales training book. But he's so deep in the weeds that he's talking about proposals now!" Guilty as charged. But the reason I must include proposals here is that just a few small tweaks to proposals can have a tremendous impact on your sales organization as a whole. I can't, in good conscience, leave this out. You can have your sales team implement these changes so easily— and you'll see a massive uptick in sales as a result.

Let's get right to it. Here are five keys to the most successful sales proposal:

1. **The sales proposal always comes after a thorough CUPBAN disqualification conversation. It never comes before.**

   This is so critical that I put it first. Your salespeople should never give a prospect a proposal until they thoroughly understand what's going on in the prospect's world. This has to become company policy. The beauty of this policy is that it forces your salespeople to do a good job in the discovery phase of the sales process.

   There are no exceptions to this rule. Even if a prospect says early on, "Can you just send me a proposal?" it must be company policy that your salespeople can never put together a quote or proposal before having a thorough disqualification conversation. This is easier than it sounds. Simply have your salespeople respond, "I'd love to put together a proposal for you, but I just don't know enough about your situation yet to be able to craft something that would be useful. Would it be OK if I asked you a few questions before we get to that?"

Then your salespeople can take the prospect right back into the CUPBAN disqualification questions.

2. The sales proposal lays out the discussed challenges and objectives from the disqualification conversation.

Typically, every sales proposal should lay out at least three key challenges and objectives that were discussed during the disqualification conversation. This creates a proposal that shows the salesperson truly understands what's going on in the world of the prospect. By this measure, it can't be boilerplate. Instead, it's a customized summary of what was specifically discussed between salesperson and prospect.

The value of solving the prospect's challenges and achieving objectives should be at least 10 times the cost of the solution.

This requires that the salesperson has had a deep conversation with the prospect not only about challenges, but also about key objectives. In particular, the proposal should show clear understanding of the prospect's top three objectives. The start of any strong proposal includes a reference to these objectives, which will help it stand apart from your competitors' proposals.

3. The sales proposal restates the value of achieving those objectives and solving those challenges.

Remember the upside step of CUPBAN? Every sales proposal should restate the value that was established during that phase of the sales process. Again, this step helps your salespeople provide context for the sale, so that the fee for the offering will seem almost inconsequential.

What's more, the value of solving the prospect's challenges and achieving objectives should be at least 10 times the cost of the solution. For that marketing company solving a $10 million problem, a $500,000 solution will seem inconsequential. This is where your salespeople will create huge value in the eyes of their prospects. Restating this value in the proposal makes it a logical next step for the prospect to work with your company.

The number of product options heavily influences buying behaviors.

4. The sales proposal provides three options for accomplishing objectives.

Every proposal your salespeople send out should provide at least three options for accomplishing the prospect's objectives. The vast majority of proposals today only give one option to the prospect. This is a massive lost opportunity. No matter how strong your salespeople's disqualification meetings are, they simply can't read the prospect's mind. It's impossible to know exactly what a prospect wants. That's why it's so important to provide three options for working with your organization. Here's what I mean:

- **Option 1:** A more basic, less expensive option that's still profitable to your organization.

- **Option 2:** A middle-of-the-road option that would probably be your core offering for the majority of prospects to choose.

- **Option 3:** A high-end option that's the truly premium choice.

By setting up the proposal this way, your salespeople provide context for the prospect to make a decision. The power of that premium option isn't just that some prospects will actually choose it. It also sets the bar high, making the middle option seem like a bargain. This three-option approach will help your sales team make larger sales and close more sales just by giving people the freedom to choose.

The data supports this. A recent study published in the *Harvard Business Review* showed that the number of product options heavily influences buying behaviors. In the study, when just one option was given, only 10% of buyers purchased. But when two options were shown, 66% of buyers agreed to purchase.[96]

What's more, when buyers are given a low-level option, a middle option, and a premium option, this creates a kind of "relative positioning" that makes the middle option more popular.

Whether you realize it or not, this is a phenomenon you've witnessed firsthand at many restaurants. Research shows that the second-most-expensive bottle of wine is frequently purchased as most restaurants, as is the second-cheapest. Why? Buying the second-most-expensive bottle makes customers feel like they're getting something nice—but not over-the-top. Buying the second-cheapest bottle makes customers feel like they're getting a good deal—but not being cheap.[97]

5. The sales proposal doubles as a basic contract.

Many organizations require serious contracts, and that's fine. But if possible, make your proposals signable. Every proposal that your salespeople create should serve as a basic contract, too. There should be a clear space where the prospect can sign to start the project. Remember, every time your salespeople add additional steps to the sales process, they create opportunities for the sale to fall apart. If someone has to first approve the proposal, and then it takes a week to put together the contract, there's more likelihood every day that the prospect might have a change of heart and do something else.

> *Suppliers who make buying easy are 62% likelier than their competitors to win a high-quality sale where the buyer chooses a premium option.*

In fact, research shows that suppliers who make buying easy are 62% likelier than their competitors to win a high-quality sale where the buyer chooses a premium option.[98] So, your salespeople should always give prospects the opportunity to sign the proposal as the first step to doing business with your company. Make sure all proposals serve as a contract, understanding it may not be legally binding, but just as a first step to get the ball rolling.

PRESENTATIONS

Sales presentations matter. Buyers rank them as one of the most important factors in their buying process, making them a crucial part of the sales cycle.[99] Depending on the type of offering you have, your salespeople might send over the proposal before the presentation, or vice versa. They might be presenting the proposal face-to-face or sending it via email. There are many different ways to do what's appropriate for your company's offering.

In an ideal world, though, your salespeople will share the proposal in the presentation. Of course, the caveat is that if your proposals are highly complex, your salespeople can send them over ahead of time and just present the key pieces in the presentation. Here, we'll focus on four components you can institutionalize to make sure your salespeople's presentations are the most effective they can possibly be.

1. **Only present to the challenges that the prospect mentioned.**

Buyers rank presentations as one of the most important factors in their buying process.

There's a tendency for salespeople to show the entire offering when presenting to the prospect. That's how we get 40-page proposals and two-hour-long presentations. No prospect wants that. Instead, prospects want your salespeople to answer the simple question, "Are you going to solve my problems?" All they care about is solving the challenges that are holding them back, so they can achieve their objectives. It's imperative that your salespeople stop presenting every bell and whistle and instead only present directly to the challenges the prospect mentioned during discovery.

This will require reinforcement to ensure your sales team is truly customizing its presentations for each prospect. The top two ways that your salespeople can better serve prospects, according to research, are to understand their needs and present relevant information.[100]

2. Use a case study approach.

In 1887, National Cash Register created what became known as the NCR Primer. This was the first formalized selling process, and it essentially taught a variation of the feature and benefit selling approach. Salespeople were instructed to show a feature of their offering, and then state a benefit of that feature.

I know this firsthand because my father learned to sell at NCR. He would tell me stories about having to memorize three hours of canned presentation that he'd then have to pitch to each prospect. Of course, this approach is completely outdated today. But amazingly, most salespeople still use the basic feature and benefit style of presenting.

Instead, they should use a case study approach to presentations, showing real-life examples that illustrate how your company's offering has helped other clients in similar situations. If your salespeople can show buyers how others similar

Your organization should develop at least five case studies for your sales team to use.

to them have experienced positive results from purchasing your product or service, they will be much more likely to buy.[101]

Your organization should develop at least five case studies for your sales team to use. These case studies will show the challenges the prospect faced, what your company did to solve those challenges, and what the results of that work turned out to be.

Specific results should always be included—that means real numbers or other outcomes that can be objectively quantified. When your salespeople frame their presentations with these engaging case studies, they tell prospects a story as opposed to just rattling off a boring, run-of-the-mill presentation on the features and benefits of the offering.

3. Get feedback throughout.

Most sales presentations are monologues that can go on for hours without the salesperson having any clue how the prospect feels. This is a disaster. The least successful presentations tend to have long, uninterrupted pitches that can last as long as 106 seconds. In fact, in a recent analysis of sales presentations, researchers failed to find a single presentation that led to a closed deal that involved more than 76 seconds of uninterrupted pitching.[102]

During a presentation, your salespeople should use feedback loops at least 50 times.

To avoid this, have your salespeople engage prospects throughout their presentations with little feedback loops. These are brief questions used to create feedback and buy-in, and they've been shown to significantly increase persuasiveness when the presenter is perceived as credible.[103]

Your salespeople can ask simple questions like: "Does that make sense? Can you see what I'm saying here? Does this apply to your organization?" These questions will help your salespeople keep a pulse on how the presentation is going, while making it a dialogue that truly engages the prospect. In addition, this process makes prospects feel like they've participated in defining the benefits that can be obtained by making the purchase. Research shows that this leads to a stronger commitment and sense of urgency to complete the purchase.[104]

> *Top-performing reps get 28% more questions from prospects during presentations than average performers.*

Does that make sense? (See what I just did there—I asked you for feedback, and you might have nodded.) During a presentation, your salespeople should use feedback loops at least 50 times. No, that number's not a typo. This approach can be easily taught to your salespeople through trainings in sales meetings, and it's such a powerful change. Can you see that?

4. Present less.

The simple mantra "present less" can dramatically increase the effectiveness of your sales team. Data shows that star reps give their prospects just enough information to spark curiosity and provoke questions. As a result, top-performing reps get 28%

more questions from prospects during presentations than average performers.[105]

If we were to break down the typical sales process that most salespeople follow, we'd find that presentations take up about 80% of the process. That's no good.

We want to flip that statistic on its head, so that 80% of the sales process is spent on the disqualification phase, and only 20% is spent on the presentation. Sales presentations should just be about presenting as little information as needed in order to enable the prospect to make an informed decision. The amount of information prospects truly need to see is always less than what the salesperson thinks. Remember, your salespeople should only present to the challenges mentioned during disqualification.

As you can see, we covered some really tactical pieces of the presentation phase. But as much as it's tactical, it's also part of a management and leadership mindset that should manifest in all aspects of your organization.

53% of customer loyalty isn't the result of your product, company, or service, but rather the behaviors your salespeople use when selling.

The disqualification process is far more important than the presentation—whereas at most organizations today, it's the complete opposite. By having your salespeople make this switch, you'll see a huge increase in sales, and a marked uptick in the effectiveness and efficiency of your sales team.

ACCOUNT MANAGEMENT

Because this isn't a sales training book, I'm not going to get too deep into account management strategies. The reality is that effective account management and client retention hinge on both organizational priorities and the behaviors of your salespeople. In fact, 53% of customer loyalty isn't the result of your product, company, or service, but rather the behaviors your salespeople use when selling.[106]

Your sales team can use the CUPBAN process with existing clients as well as with prospects. The key is to get your salespeople to *want* to understand what's going on in the lives of their clients.

Account management can be viewed as an extension of CUPBAN, only applied to existing clients. Think about the cost of acquiring new clients at your organization. If you don't know the cost, do the math. It's the total sum you spend annually to acquire new clients, divided by the number of new clients you actually acquire:

Total Cost for Acquiring a New Client

Marketing Cost to Acquire a New Client:

A. Total cost of marketing geared toward acquiring new clients in the past year: $_____

Labor Cost to Acquire a New Client:

B. Percent of time you expected your salespeople to spend prospecting, meeting with new prospects, working on presentations, and following up with prospects (all new sales activity) in the past year: _____%

C. What was the annual labor cost for your sales team (total amount, including base salaries, commissions and benefits)? $_____

D. Now multiply line B by line C (remember that B is a percent): $_____

E. Now add line A and line D together: _____

This is your total expenditure for acquiring new clients.

F. Number of new clients acquired in the past year:

_____

Finally, divide line E by line F: $_____

 You can download a free PDF version of this template in my Key Pages & Worksheets Guide at www.MarcWayshak.com/HighVelocity.

This is your approximate cost for bringing on each new client. Chances are, that number is pretty painful. It should give you newfound appreciation for the value of selling more to existing clients.

Selling more to existing clients isn't magic. People always ask me, "Can you provide us with cross-selling or upselling strategies?" My simple response is, "You don't need a fancy strategy. You just need to apply the CUPBAN process to your existing clients."

This is the only strategy your salespeople need for account management.

There's a high chance that your salespeople and account managers don't use a formal process like CUPBAN with their existing clients.

In fact, over half of all salespeople report that their ability to penetrate new business units in an existing client account needs improvement—or even a total overhaul.[107]

This means that your salespeople likely don't know much about what their clients are looking to accomplish. The simplest way to sell deeper to existing clients is to have your salespeople take them through the CUPBAN process on a continual basis. That's it.

One of the best ways to do this is to conduct regular "business reviews" with current clients. One of my clients recently formalized this process, having their account managers set up quarterly business reviews with all of their key clients. Each salesperson has 10 key accounts with A-level clients. These salespeople are expected to set at least one business review meeting with each of those key clients every quarter.

> 7 out of 10 consumers—and a whopping 82% of business buyers—say that technology has made it easier to take their business elsewhere.

In doing so, they can find out what's new with the client, dig into their top challenges, and find out what's changed at the organization. This is the only strategy your salespeople need for account management. It's not fancy. It's just about taking the time to understand their existing clients.

A note on retention...for clients

The process I described above is also a client retention strategy. Since your clients have more access to information than ever before, it's never been easier for them to leave. In fact, 7 out of 10 consumers—and a whopping 82%

of business buyers—say that technology has made it easier to take their business elsewhere.[108]

One of the most common reasons clients leave an existing supplier or vendor is that the vendor ultimately didn't care enough about them. It's as simple as that. If your salespeople conduct those quarterly meetings to understand what the client needs and wants, you'll more effectively retain clients.

You don't have to spend more money on retention. Just have your salespeople focus the same CUPBAN selling strategies on existing clients. This will not only help to retain those key accounts, but also to grow them. You can't spend all your time and money on acquiring new clients if you're just bleeding out old accounts as you go. That sounds reminiscent of Sisyphus pushing the boulder up the hill, doesn't it? Instead, use the same CUPBAN approach on both sides of business: old and new. Grow both as a way to increase your market share. Don't use one as a way to compensate for the loss of the other.

Section III

Infrastructure

WE TALKED ABOUT Alexander the Great earlier in this book. The military strategy laid out by his father, Philip, was integral to Alexander's success as world conqueror. Without it, he never would have vanquished his enemies and destroyed the Persian Empire.

But when Alexander died suddenly at the age of 32, all of his achievements were quickly undone.

First, a series of bloody civil wars broke out. Over the course of the next 50 years, Alexander's former generals and family members vied to control different parts of his sprawling empire. Within the span of just one generation, the massive empire he built had splintered and disintegrated.

What was missing? Alexander had the strategy—and no doubt, he taught his top generals and close relatives everything he knew. What he lacked, however, was the infrastructure to support the empire after he was gone. He left no apparent heir or appointed successor. There were no directions for how the empire should be ruled in his absence. Everything fell apart.

Rome, on the other hand, never had a general like Alexander. Even so, it remained the uncontested ruler of Europe for more than 400 years.

What set the Roman Empire apart was simple: It may not have had the best generals in the world, but it had the best infrastructure. All of Rome's systems—government, politics, roads, information networks, and more—were built to function not under the rule of one man, but for the greater good of a vast empire.

Simply put, Romans mastered the day-to-day administration of who was supposed to do what, where, and when. Not only that, they mastered infrastructure on a colossal scale, successfully governing millions of people from disparate nations who spoke different languages, prayed to different gods, and cared about different things. No one has done it better since.

And so, even with the best sales strategy, your organization will fail to thrive without the right infrastructure in place. You might be an Alexander the Great, with a proven strategy under your belt, sterling leadership skills, and charisma to boot. But just because the strategy works for you, that doesn't mean every member of your team can do it, too. Your salespeople need systems to follow, management to rely on, and accountability to face. That's infrastructure.

Romans mastered the day-to-day administration of who was supposed to do what, where, and when.

In sales, infrastructure is the intersection of sales leadership, CRM practices, and accountability processes to drive day-to-day sales activity. These are the critical systems that bring together your people and your strategy. Without it, success is haphazard and irreplicable.

I'd like to kick off this section on infrastructure by giving you some insight into my own business. As a sales strategist, I work with senior leaders to develop the strategy to dramatically increase sales. Yet, more often than not, when senior leaders reach out to me looking for help with their sales organizations, the first thing they say is: "I want to talk to you about sales training."

> *Sales training alone simply will not solve the issues faced by the vast majority of sales organizations today.*

Before responding to this directly, I always ask a bunch of questions to determine what's really going on at the organization. I ask about the amount of activity their salespeople are conducting. I ask about their close rates. I ask about the sales team's overall adoption of CRM, about the sales leadership structure at the company, and about the effectiveness of their sales managers. I ask about the role the CEO plays in sales. In almost every single case, the answers to these questions build a clear picture, which is: Sales training alone is not the answer to solving their problems.

Sales training alone simply will not solve the issues faced by the vast majority of sales organizations today. I always tell my clients, "Look, I could come in and do some sales training at your organization. And I could knock it out of the park. But within two or three weeks, every single person on your sales team will be back to doing exactly what they were doing before I came in. There will be zero difference. This will remain the case forever if your organization never changes its sales infrastructure." In fact, research shows that up to 90% of all sales training has no positive impact after the training is done.[109]

Chances are, since you've made it this far into my book, you see my point. If you brought me—or any other sales expert—into your organization just to do training for a day or two, you'd quickly realize that it wouldn't lead to any real, lasting change. Your managers would go right back to tracking (or failing to track) their numbers the way they were before; your salespeo-

Up to 90% of all sales training has no positive impact after the training is done.

ple would continue to sell the way they were selling before; your senior leadership would continue to lead without any meaningful change to their approach.

Pretty soon, this scenario begins to look a lot like Einstein's definition of insanity: Doing the same thing over and over again and expecting different results. If we don't augment the behavior that's creating problems in the first place, we'll never achieve sustainable change. Period.

That's what this section of the book is all about: implementing the right sales infrastructure to enable lasting change at your organization. Before you can build a house, you need a solid foundation. Infrastructure is the foundation of your sales organization. Without it, everything will crumble.

The reason this is the third section in the book is pretty simple: Infrastructure is the framework that holds together the other two components of a high-velocity sales organization—the sales performers themselves, and the sales strategy they use. Think of your sales organization as a house with old beams. You can't fully replace all the beams in the house—that would be far too expensive and time-consuming. But what you can do is reinforce those beams. You can add more beams. You can bring in a top contractor to assess where the weakest beams are, and how to best fortify them. That's exactly what the right sales infrastructure does.

Without performers and strategy in place, there's nothing to reinforce with infrastructure.

As we go through this section, I'll continually draw your attention back to earlier chapters of this book. Why? Because everything in sales is interconnected: Without performers and strategy in place, there's nothing to reinforce with infrastructure.

In the following pages, we'll forge ahead and start talking about the main tenets of a strong sales infrastructure, including exactly how to foster discipline around the sales strategy, and how to ensure that the right people are doing the right things.

But first, a little disclaimer...

If you're looking for a highly complex, ultra-sophisticated approach to sales infrastructure, this isn't the book for you. I'm all about simplicity. Over many years working with organizations of all sizes, I've found that the simpler the infrastructure, the better. The real key to successful sales infrastructure isn't about implementing a fancy approach. It's about building discipline throughout your sales organization. That starts at the very top, by determining which indicators you want to measure—in a meaningful way, on a consistent basis, to track sales efforts. This makes all the difference between infrastructure success or failure.

The importance of discipline might sound obvious, but so many CEOs and VPs of sales struggle with it. Instead, they have a "flavor of the month" mentality when it comes to sales, always looking for a new approach or a sexier solution to share with the sales team.

If this sounds like you, I strongly encourage you to break that pattern. Stop constantly looking for a fancy new sales approach and focus instead on building real discipline around the simple approaches I'm about to share with you. Discipline is the only thing that will create true adoption throughout the ranks of your sales team.

> *The real key to successful sales infrastructure isn't about implementing a fancy approach. It's about building discipline throughout your sales organization.*

Not convinced? Just think about the process of training a dog. If you learn a bunch of new approaches from a dog trainer, but forget to use them consistently with your dog a few days after you start, what happens? Inevitably, your dog is far less likely to listen to you. He's confused by your lack of consistency, and the new lessons you taught him quickly become muddled—did they really matter, or not?

The same thing is true for your sales team. If your salespeople perceive that every new sales approach you introduce is "just another phase," then nothing will ever be successful. Your sales strategy must be consistently reinforced with a highly disciplined approach. Now, let's explore how to do just that.

Chapter 7:

Sales Leadership

IF YOU THINK of sales infrastructure as one of those old food pyramids, where the most important part of the diet is at the top, then sales leadership would be the most dominant food group—by far.

Leadership is all about your sales management structure and choosing the right people to fill those management roles. This is critical. The first step is to determine what your own role is. Where do you fit into your organization's sales leadership? The answer to this question depends upon many factors, such as how big your organization is, whether it's a startup or an established company, and whether there are levels of management in place below you at the organization.

I can't answer these particular questions for you. However, I can tell you that the single most important factor is the size of your sales team.

Even the most talented sales managers "cap out" in terms of effectiveness at around seven direct reports. If you have only one manager with eight or more direct reports, then that manager isn't even managing. Instead, that manager is merely putting out fires and barely holding it together. There's very little actual sales support or coaching that one person can provide to that many salespeople.

So, if your sales team is larger than seven, you need to have at least one manager for every seven salespeople. If your sales team is smaller than seven, the question is: Are you the one managing the sales team? Or do you bring in an outsider to do it?

Even the most talented sales managers "cap out" in terms of effectiveness at around seven direct reports.

Those answers depend on the profitability of your organization, and where you are in the company's lifecycle. If your organization is a startup and you're reading this book to help build out a brand new sales team, then it probably makes sense for you to manage the sales team yourself—at least at first. The only caveat, of course, is if you have no discipline, or if you acknowledge that you're just not good at managing people.

On the other hand, if your organization is on the larger side, and it's been around for a while, you probably have existing levels of management below you. In that case, it makes more sense for you to hire an outsider to manage and run your sales organization.

But here's the kicker: It's incredibly difficult to hire great sales managers. As in, one of the most challenging things to do at any sales-driven organization. Let's talk about why that is.

There are two types of salespeople out there: Those who are great, and those who aren't.

HIRING SALES MANAGERS

Sales management is markedly different from other types of management, and for good reason. In industries other than sales, such as finance or operations, the cream always rises to the top. The best performers in those fields tend to eventually find themselves in senior roles, leading and managing others. But this simply isn't the case for sales.

There are two types of salespeople out there: Those who are great, and those who aren't. If you're great at sales, then why move into management? You can make more money as a salesperson than you can as a sales manager. So why do it?

The answer is that salespeople often move into management positions because, deep down, they're not entirely comfortable with selling. This, of course, isn't always the case. But in general, this category of salespeople bill themselves as highly effective sales managers—but really, they're just failed salespeople. They can talk the talk, but they can't walk the walk. This is the main reason it's so challenging to hire for the position of sales manager.

What's more, while you can use the hiring process to determine a salesperson's effectiveness, and you can use the online assessment to measure cognitive ability, there's no way to truly test for sales management talent. Instead, you have to rely much more on references and previous experience. It's like throwing a dart in the dark, and just hoping it hits.

In addition, this level of recruit is notoriously difficult to retain. One study found that more than half of senior organizational leaders are engaged in active job searches, while 94% of VPs are willing to take a call from a recruiter.[110]

I don't say this to scare you away from hiring outsiders to manage your sales team. I've seen it work many times. But you need to bring a critical eye to that process. If you're going to bring in an outsider to a sales management role, you must be incredibly discerning about the following four factors:

1. What type of person you're looking to hire

2. Exactly what that person's role will entail

3. The three key objectives of that person's position

4. How you will align those objectives with compensation

More than half of senior organizational leaders are engaged in active job searches, while 94% of VPs are willing to take a call from a recruiter.

Types of sales management

Let's say you've decided to hire an outsider for a sales management role. What will that role look like? There are really only three types of sales management at any organization. Here they are:

1. Sales executive.

This person usually holds a title such as CSO, VP of sales, or director of sales. The sales executive brings a real vision and strategy to your sales organization. If you make the decision to hire a sales executive, this will be one of the most important

> *The sales executive brings a real vision and strategy to your sales organization.*

hiring moves you ever make at your organization. The success of your entire company depends upon the success of this person in that role.

Is your sales executive going to hire the right managers and salespeople? Will he or she create a positive sales culture? Is your sales executive not only likeable, but also disciplined? You wouldn't believe how many organizations bring me in simply because their sales executive lacks discipline. This can be disastrous for morale on the sales team and lead to real issues with profitability for the organization.

2. Sales manager.

One level down from the sales executive, sales managers focus on executing strategy on the front lines with salespeople. Not as much part of the "big picture" strategy, managers are out there implementing sales initiatives, coaching salespeople, and holding them accountable on a daily basis. At some smaller organizations, the roles of sales executive and sales manager might be filled by the same person.

At larger organizations, though, it makes more sense to have the sales executive do less front-line work, while the sales manager focuses on day-to-day execution. And as I mentioned before, no single sales manager should ever be managing more than seven people. Otherwise, they're just going to be holding everything together but never doing any real proactive development of their salespeople.

3. Sales leader.

The sales leader is essentially the player-coach. Sales leaders both sell and coach other salespeople. Most sales leaders just fall into these roles, either because they were one of the top performers on the team, or because they were tapped on the shoulder to lead. Maybe their compensation was even increased so they would take on more of a management role. Sales leaders have to carry their own direct numbers while simultaneously managing other salespeople. This is often tricky.

This is one of the more precarious leadership roles. Essentially, you're taking your top-performing salesperson out of the field and putting that person into a role that's not a natural fit.

Sales leaders have to carry their own direct numbers while simultaneously managing other salespeople. This is often tricky.

If you absolutely must have a sales leader at your organization, it should only be in the capacity of a 1:1 or 1:2 relationship, where one sales leader mentors one or two salespeople in what's often referred to as a "pod structure." Sales leaders should never have a large team of people under them, unless the subordinates are in very specialized roles that directly support the sales leader.

NO MORE DOTTED LINES

Now that we've laid out the three types of sales management, let's talk about how they come together. The key point here is that your sales management structure should be as simple as possible.

I know the word "simple" has been cropping up all over this section, and that will continue. The importance of simplicity can't be overstated when it comes to sales management. Here, simplicity means that it should be abundantly clear who reports to whom, and who is accountable for whom. There should be zero crossover in terms of who reports directly to the sales executive versus the sales manager.

I can't tell you the number of times I'm brought into an organization to develop sales infrastructure and I see an organizational chart like this:

PREVIOUS SALES ORG CHART

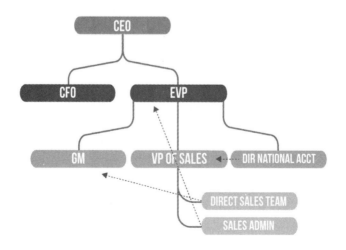

What a mess. Notice the dotted lines that indicate all the "secondary" lines of accountability among salespeople and their superiors. Those dotted lines are crushing. Where there's no clear accountability, there's no accountability at all. And accountability is everything in sales, as we'll see in the next chapter.

To ensure accountability and eradicate confusion, your sales management structure must be completely devoid of dotted lines, like the organizational chart below. Map out exactly what your sales organization looks like, in a simple way, with nothing but direct reports.

SIMPLIFIED SALES ORG CHART

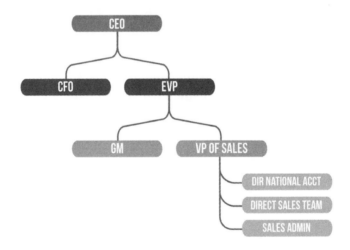

Sales leadership compensation

Once your sales organization structure is in place, now we align incentives for each of those sales leadership positions. The variable compensation for a sales executive or manager should depend directly on the effectiveness of the people below them. This means that all incentives encourage the manager or executive to increase the effectiveness of those under them. In turn, this will ultimately help them achieve their own goals.

There are no hard and fast rules when it comes to sales leadership compensation. It will vary dramatically by organization and industry, but ultimately there are three key factors that should go into determining variable compensation:

1. Overall company sales

2. Overall company profitability (if it's within the control of sales leadership)

3. Sales growth

Any other objectives aren't key objectives—they're merely tertiary.

Chapter 8:

Sales Team Compensation

WE'VE DISCUSSED COMPENSATION as it relates to sales management. But what about your salespeople? Sales team compensation is one of the most crucial components of sales infrastructure. At the same time, it's one of the most controversial topics in boardroom discussions. In fact, 85% of companies will change their sales compensation plan this year.[111]

When compensation structure is set up properly, it creates a direct alignment of incentives for the sales team. When a salesperson does what you want, that salesperson is compensated appropriately for that work. This is what a good compensation plan does.

On the other hand, bad compensation plans can lead to the total destruction of a sales organization. I've seen many cases where sales organizations bleed talent as a direct result of introducing poorly thought-out, untested compensation structures that make salespeople angry.

But it's important to note that—while they're crucial—compensation structures aren't the only factor in attracting and retaining top talent at your sales organization. Having a sales culture that's supportive and exciting will also make a tremendous impact. According to research by Glassdoor, 71% of sales professionals are likely to accept less money to work at a company with a great culture.[112]

85% of companies will change their sales compensation plan this year.

In fact, my own research shows that company culture and management effectiveness are the two most important factors for salespeople when selecting a sales job, closely followed by commission.[113] Keep that in mind as we go through this section.

That said, this chapter is all about how to build the best possible compensation structure for your sales team. Let's start out with a high-level view of the three core concepts behind any great sales compensation plan:

1. Your sales superstars should become very rich.

The point here is simple: If there are sales superstars at your organization, then a great compensation structure will make them very rich. If those superstars don't get rich, then there's something wrong with your plan.

The data says it all: 38% of salespeople who sell for above-market compensation companies rated their sales leadership as excellent, compared to only 2% of salespeople at below-average-market compensation companies.[114] Now, it's possible that there isn't a sales superstar on your team today. When I say sales superstar, I mean someone who is absolutely dominant on your sales team.

Let me give you the example of Bill, a superstar salesperson at one of my client organizations. Bill worked on a sales team of 10 people. The company revenues were $40 million, and Bill's personal direct sales were $20 million. He carried the weight of nine other salespeople. He also out-earned the CEO of the company, bringing home close to $1 million a year.

> *38% of salespeople who sell for above-market compensation companies rated their sales leadership as excellent, compared to only 2% of salespeople at below-average-market compensation companies.*

As a result, Bill got amazing perks, like a full-time sales assistant and stock in the company. Quite frankly, had the CEO dropped dead, it would have had less of an impact on the company than if something had happened to Bill. That's how important Bill was.

The CEO of Bill's company was savvy and smart. He set aside his ego, because he recognized how vital Bill was to the success of the organization. He was happy to see Bill make more money than he did, and supported Bill however he could.

This is not an obvious point. Ego has no place in compensation structure. I can't tell you the number of times I see companies cap compensation at the top, saying, "That salesperson is making way too much money, so we should change the plan."

> *Ego has no place in compensation structure.*

Most of the time, this is ego-driven. Management realizes that a salesperson makes more than they do, and they simply won't have it. Just the other day I got a call from a recently hired VP of sales who was freaking out because the top salesperson in the organization earned considerably more than he did, and he thought that was "inappropriate."

The only thing I considered inappropriate about this was that the VP of sales was worried about a salesperson earning more than he did. As I said before, there is no place for ego in compensation structure. Don't cap your salespeople's salaries. Let them earn more than you. Be psyched when they do. Sales superstars are a true gift that many organizations don't have. Any great compensation structure will make those superstars incredibly wealthy.

2. You must do it right the first time around.

Do-overs come at too high a cost when it comes to sales compensation. If you introduce a plan only to change it six months later, sales morale will inevitably plummet. Nothing makes salespeople more insecure—or angry—than thinking they're about to get screwed over by management. It's crucial that you take the time to carefully plan out your new sales compensation structure before introducing it to your team. Do it right the first time around.

3. Your plan must pass the back-of-the-envelope test.

Unsurprisingly, the best sales compensation structures are the simplest ones. Your salespeople must be able to understand the ins and outs of the plan, right off the bat. This can be a real challenge. Very few organizations have compensation plans that can literally fit on the back of an envelope—but that's exactly what you want.

When I help my clients cut out all the fat and simplify their compensation plans to the fullest, I call this "passing the back-of-the-envelope test." This is critical because compensation is all about alignment of incentives. Encouraging people with the carrot of more money will only work if your salespeople understand the plan. When there's confusion about a compensation structure, it never works.

> *Unsurprisingly, the best sales compensation structures are the simplest ones.*

I also find many salespeople to be highly conspiratorial. Simplicity mitigates conspiracy theories. Ensure that your compensation structure focuses only on a few key indicators of success to drive the needle forward. Your salespeople should easily be able to fill in the following blanks:

"If I do _____, then I will make $_____."

or

"If I do _____, _____, and _____, then I will make $_____."

YOUR TARGET-AT-PLAN

When putting together your new sales compensation structure, there's a clear first place to start: the Target-at-Plan. Once you've clarified your Target-at-Plan, you'll have a solid foundation for the nuts and bolts of the rest of the structure. Your Target-at-Plan answers this question: What are you willing to pay your salespeople for producing what you want them to realistically produce?

In other words, you'll need to fill in the following blanks:

"I'm willing to pay $_____ if a salesperson can produce $_____."

For example, you might pay $100,000 to a salesperson who can produce $1 million, if your goal is to get salespeople to realistically sell $1 million. Don't be stingy here. Of course, you need to make sure your organization can make money—but this isn't the place to get tight with your purse strings. The choices you make regarding your

Target-at-Plan will have long-lasting consequences on your ability to recruit top sales talent to your organization.

BASE VS. VARIABLE COMPENSATION

Once you've established your Target-at-Plan, it's time to break down your base vs. variable compensation numbers. I've always been a proponent of keeping base compensation as low as possible, while making variable compensation very, very generous. Having said that, great salespeople won't work at a company if the base compensation is too low. They want to see that an organization is willing to carry them even when they're not making the company money early on.

The simplest way to determine base compensation is to figure out the standard base salary in your industry—and use that. Don't overthink it. Then, to determine variable compensation, just subtract the base salary from your Target-at-Plan.

Let's say your Target-at-Plan is $100,000 and your industry's standard base is $60,000. That means a commission of $40,000 is left over. What kind of incentives can you use to encourage the right behavior, so your salespeople earn what they need to earn in order to get that commission? In other words, what kind of commission structures should you put in place?

There are two basic types of sales commission structures you can use:

1. Commission based on top-line sales revenues

2. Commission based on gross profitability of sales

Without question, the simplest approach is to pay commission based on top-line sales revenues. But this is one case where simpler doesn't always equal better.

If your organization has a challenge with gross profitability—for example, your salespeople are consistently closing low-profit sales—then the best approach is to pay commission based on gross profitability of sales, assuming it's easy to calculate.

A word of fair warning: Paying commission based on gross profitability can get complicated. However, when done well, it can single-handedly solve many sales profitability problems.

Let me give you an example. I had a client who brought me in to help with commission structure. At the time, they were paying 12% commission on top-line sales revenues. But due to extreme pricing pressures in the industry, their salespeople were closing business at very low profit margins. The company was essentially making zero profit off of sales.

My first order of business was to shift their model immediately to a commission based on 30% of gross profitability of sales. So, instead of getting 12% of the top-line revenues of sales they made, salespeople were now getting 30% of the gross profits of those sales. This changed everything. Pretty much overnight, the salespeople became experts on sales profitability, changing their behavior to achieve higher profit margins.

A word of fair warning: Paying commission based on gross profitability can get complicated.

Before we made this shift to commission based on gross profitability, the company's CEO had spent years constantly complaining to the sales team, but there had never been any change in behavior. This case is the perfect example of how a simple shift in commission structure can solve some dire business challenges, while kicking the sales team into high gear.

OBJECTIVE-BASED BONUSES

On top of commission, many organizations effectively use bonuses to drive other objectives. For example, you can pay bonuses to your salespeople every time they achieve key objectives. This approach to commission is particularly effective for incentivizing your top salespeople to aim even higher.

As long as they don't get too convoluted, objective-based bonuses can be a powerful driver of positive results in sales. Here are a few objective-based bonus structures that work well:

- **Sale size:** Salespeople get a bonus when they close particularly large sales.

- **Number of sales closed:** Salespeople get a bonus when they close a certain number of sales per month, or per period.

- **Profitability targets:** Salespeople get a bonus when they achieve a certain level of profitability in sales.

- **Sales activity:** Salespeople get a bonus when they exceed a certain number of sales meetings.

- **Short-term, specific achievement:** Salespeople get a bonus when they accomplish a desired outcome during a specific period.

Of course, you need to choose objectives that matter to you. For example, if sale size isn't that important to you, then it shouldn't be a factor in your bonus structure.

Objective-based bonuses can be a powerful driver of positive results in sales.

Finally, it's important to note that bonuses should never be based on subjective ideas such as "doing a great job" or "personal improvement." Because these types of bonuses are impossible to measure, most organizations feel compelled to give them out. Thus, it becomes deferred compensation rather than a true performance-based bonus.

Notice that I haven't suggested anywhere in this section that you should cap your salespeople's commissions at a certain number. I'll say it again: Caps are crushing to sales organizations. From my perspective, caps are almost always the direct result of a sales outsider stepping in and asking, purely out of ego, "Why are these salespeople making so much money?" There's simply no place for that mindset in a high-velocity sales organization.

TRY TO GAME YOUR OWN PLAN

Once you have your sales compensation structure written out, it's time to try to game your own plan. Sit down with someone who's great with numbers, such as your accountant or your CFO. Run calculations to try to beat your own plan. Search for loopholes. Try to take advantage of the structure. Run at least 10 simulations of your plan with scenarios ranging from your bottom performers to your top performers, including all those folks in the middle. Plug all their numbers into the structure just to make sure your plan is really what you think it is.

I promise you, if holes exist in your compensation structure, your salespeople will find them. They're either going to take advantage of those holes—or they'll be really angry with management, thinking that the holes in the plan were intentional to somehow take advantage of them.

The other benefit of trying to game your own plan is that you can test out the simplicity of your compensation structure. Ultimately, you're going to have to administer this plan to the entire sales team. You're going to have to pay your salespeople based on this plan. By testing it out, you can avoid a lot of self-inflicted pain. Make sure it's simple and easy to administer.

> *I promise you, if holes exist in your compensation structure, your salespeople will find them.*

I've seen so many well-intentioned compensation plans turn ugly—to the point where CFOs are ripping out their hair in frustration—just because a plan hasn't been thoroughly tested. Don't make that mistake.

Chapter 9:

Accountability

IF YOUR SALES infrastructure is the foundation of your sales organization, then accountability is the mortar that holds your sales infrastructure together. Accountability means different things to different people, so let me give you my definition: Accountability is the direct measurement of what a salesperson is doing on a daily, weekly, and monthly basis in order to hit key objectives.

This is a top challenge for sales managers. Nearly half of all sales managers say productivity and performance is their biggest challenge in managing the sales team.[115]

While tracking activities is at the heart of accountability, it's not about being Big Brother. Strong accountability doesn't mean your sales managers should breathe down your salespeople's necks, constantly look over their shoulders, and second-guess their actions. Unfortunately, this is the reality at many companies. It's no wonder that 79% of all employees don't think their organization's performance review process is very good.[116]

Instead, strong accountability is about establishing a clear plan for what activities your salespeople should be doing on a regular basis—and then directly measuring those activities in order to hold them accountable. Since salespeople today spend just one-third of their day actually talking to prospects,[117] it's clear that they desperately need this help.

What's more, research shows that most average-performing salespeople make calls in the eleventh hour—making far more calls in the last month of the quarter than the first two.[118] And average sales reps only spend 36% of their time on selling tasks every day.[119] Common procrastination like this can be dramatically reduced by strong accountability systems.

Again, this is not about micromanaging salespeople. With a good accountability structure, your sales managers never have to ask pestering questions like, "What did you do today? What are you doing tomorrow? What are you going to do next week?" Strong accountability actually eradicates those conversations completely—much to the delight of managers and salespeople alike.

In order to achieve this level of accountability at your sales organization, you need to create consistent, reliable systems for measuring what your salespeople are doing. These systems provide you and your sales management with all the necessary information on the back end, through reports that are sent directly to you. No pestering conversations required.

> *Salespeople today spend just one-third of their day talking to prospects.*

THE ROLE OF YOUR CRM

Your CRM system is the backbone of sales accountability at your organization. If you're currently a CRM ninja who knows all the fanciest CRM strategies, and how to use the most advanced integration tools, then you probably won't get a lot of value out of this section. Feel free to skip it.

You won't be surprised to hear that when it comes to CRM systems, I preach simplicity above all else. I strongly believe that your CRM should be as simple as possible, so

57% of salespeople spend up to an hour per day on data entry.

it's easy for your salespeople to use, and easy for your management team to use. Both salespeople and sales managers tend to be pretty non-tech-savvy. My CRM strategy takes that into account.

Right now, your client database is likely the most important asset at your company. But is it difficult to use? Have you asked your salespeople how they feel about your current CRM system?

When I ask sales teams about this, I inevitably get a ton of eye rolls about the current processes in place. A recent study even found that 57% of salespeople spend up to an hour per day on data entry alone.[120] That's up to an hour a day spent inputting information instead of engaging with prospects or performing true selling behaviors.

When your CRM system isn't easy to use, your salespeople don't utilize it like they should. That means you don't get the information you need, and there's no accountability.

When CRM processes are challenging, many salespeople stop using the CRM altogether. They turn to spreadsheets, Google Docs, or even notebooks to track what they do. This is deadly for sales organizations. If those salespeople ever leave the company, you'll lose all that information for good. Plus, there's no way to hold sales-people accountable when they track information how they want, when they want, where they want.

57% of salespeople spend up to an hour per day on data entry alone.

If this scenario sounds familiar to you, my first suggestion is that your organization needs to adopt a sales operations mindset. This means developing an organization-wide commitment to consistently tracking and measuring important information through the CRM system. It needs to be mandatory that salespeople put all necessary information into the CRM. Keyword: *necessary*—more on this later.

That said, you shouldn't spend all your energy on compliance. Most organizations only focus on trying to get their salespeople to enter information into the CRM. But once salespeople are consistently entering that information, the company has no plan for what to do with the data. This is frustrating for salespeople, who are wasting tons of time entering data that's never even being looked at.

Among sales teams that say ineffective internal processes are their top challenge, excessive administrative tasks is the top cause.[121] It's infuriating for the sales organization, which is bending over backward to demand compliance, but then never doing anything useful with the resulting information. You don't want to be here.

The solution is to create a set of metrics that you and your sales management team can measure on a consistent basis to help forecast future sales and identify whether individual salespeople are on track to meet their goals.

Let your chosen metrics determine what information you require salespeople to enter into the CRM system.

For example, if one of the metrics you choose to measure is how many meetings your salespeople set, then you should require your salespeople to enter information about sales meetings into the CRM system.

Among sales teams that say ineffective internal processes are their top challenge, excessive administrative tasks is the top cause.

First decide what key metrics you're going to measure on a consistent basis. Then let that drive what your salespeople actually enter into the system.

We'll dive deeper into that later. For now, I'm going to lay out the most important core components of a CRM system, including what kind of information you should be pulling out and measuring. I'll also show you how to create simple CRM processes that are easy to implement and—more important—easy to create discipline around.

CRM TOOLS

Let's talk briefly about CRM tool options. Over half of all sales organizations use Salesforce—it's unequivocally the dominant CRM technology at the time of writing this book. I personally love Salesforce. I use it for my own business, and it's a fantastic tool. But for many organizations, the malleability of Salesforce can create unneeded complexity and make it more difficult to use.

If you're using Salesforce, great. But if you're not, you don't necessarily have to. There are a number of tools out there that range in price and functionality. There may be a different CRM tool that's perfect for your organization. There are two key criteria to think about when choosing your CRM:

1. **The size of your organization.**

   If you're a three-person organization and the goal is to grow to six, there are some far simpler, more basic CRM tools than Salesforce that can help you accomplish what you want. You don't necessarily need a robust, customized use of Salesforce. On the other hand, if your organization is on the larger size, Salesforce offers the best functionality and the most resources for customization on the market.

2. **The level of complexity you intend to create.**

   If you're looking to use a CRM system for its most basic functions (tracking information, sales activity, and pipeline opportunities) then there are a number of tools far cheaper and simpler than Salesforce that will allow you to accomplish that. But if you're a larger organization who needs a CRM to perfectly integrate with accounting software or other platforms, and you intend to create higher levels of complexity with your CRM, then Salesforce is going to be the best tool for you.

While choosing the right CRM tool is important, it's useless if you don't know what you should be tracking. In this section, we'll explore what metrics your CRM system should track, and how you should measure and use those metrics to assess your salespeople's progress.

Even the most basic CRM systems will track three key sales components:

1. Sales revenues

2. Sales activities

3. Sales pipelines

TRACKING SALES REVENUES

Tracking sales revenues is the simplest of these three functions. Most CRM systems send sales revenue data directly into the organization's accounting software. The problem is that organizations spend far too much time managing, measuring, and reading into those numbers.

Sales managers can use leading indicators to drive a 55% increase in relevant new-business meetings—along with a 50% reduction in onboarding time.

Simply put, sales revenues are not an accurate indicator of future sales effectiveness. In fact, they're a lagging indicator, and so they shouldn't be used to gauge whether or not a salesperson is on track to reach a goal.

Think about it this way: If one of your salespeople isn't doing what needs to be done in order to hit numbers, and you're only tracking sales revenues, then you won't know about it until the end of the month, the end of the quarter, or the end of the year. When the final numbers come in and you finally realize that the salesperson didn't reach the sales goal, it's already too late to try to get the salesperson back on track for that sales cycle.

The real challenge with lagging indicators such as sales revenues is that they don't tell us much about the future. If we spend all our time looking at sales numbers, all we're doing is looking backward.

This plays out especially clearly when organizations hire new salespeople. Organizations will often hire a new salesperson who, very quickly, gets on track to fail in the position. But since the organization is only tracking sales revenues, management has no idea until the final numbers start rolling in.

As a result, most companies end up keeping failing salespeople around for far longer than they should. I've had clients wait over two years to fire failing salespeople, simply because they weren't entirely sure that the salesperson was failing in the first place.

Instead, they should have been measuring other indicators—namely, *leading* indicators—that would have told them right away that the new salesperson wasn't on the right track. Leading indicators are essential to high-velocity sales organizations because they tell us what's going to happen in the future, as opposed to what happened in the past.

Research shows that sales managers can use leading indicators to drive a 55% increase in relevant new-business meetings—along with a 50% reduction in onboarding time.[122] In particular, there are two leading indicators I want to draw your attention to: sales activities and pipeline opportunities. High-velocity organizations spend the majority of their time measuring these two indicators to make sure their salespeople are on the right track.

TRACKING SALES ACTIVITIES

Sales activities, by definition, are the activities your salespeople do on a daily basis in order to hit their numbers. The importance of tracking these activities can't be overstated, given that most companies only track the actual sales numbers themselves. This leads to an end-of-the-month rush to close piec-

> *A staggering 81.1% of top performers spend at least 3 hours a day on sales-related activity.*

es of business, as salespeople inevitably procrastinate. The data shows that these end-of-the-month pushes coincide with a 51% decrease in overall sales win rates.[123]

One of my mentors always used to say, "What gets tracked, gets done." If we're tracking sales activities, then those activities are going to get done. In order to track sales activities properly, you need to be measuring them through your CRM system. Otherwise, your sales managers will be forced to have those pestering conversations with salespeople that make them feel micromanaged.

As long as sales activity information is going directly into the CRM system, those conversations never have to happen. You and your sales managers can simply look at the information in the system, and course-correct along the way.

Assuming you have a strong sales strategy in place, sales activity is what's going to ultimately drive sales at your organization. In other words, if your salespeople are doing the right things when selling, the only other variable that will determine success is the frequency with which they're doing those things.

The goal is to create less work for your salespeople to ensure that they actually use the system.

For example, my own research shows that while 60.8% of non-top performers spend at least 3 hours a day on sales-related activity, a staggering 81.1% of top performers spend at least 3 hours a day on sales-related activity. This means that top performers are more than 25% more likely to spend at least 3 hours a day on sales-related activity. Furthermore, salespeople who spend over 3 hours per day on sales-related activity showed an 11% increase in job satisfaction over those who spend 3 hours or less.[124]

This is why tracking sales activity is so important. Given how simple it is to track sales activity, it's astounding how few organizations do it effectively.

If your salespeople are using the CRM system as their client database, then their sales activity information should already be in the system. If it's not, it still only requires a few minor tweaks to make sure the right information is getting in there. The main requirement is that whenever your salespeople make phone calls, set sales meetings, or conduct sales meetings, that information gets put into the CRM. As long as it's going into the CRM, then management can track what every salesperson is doing on a day-to-day basis.

If your salespeople don't like to use the calendar software in the CRM, or they don't like to keep track of their calls in the CRM, then there are a number of simple tools that can help. For example, you can easily integrate your salespeople's Outlook calendars with the CRM. Whenever a salesperson creates a meeting in Outlook, that information will automatically go into the system. The goal is to create less work for your salespeople to ensure that they actually use the system in place to track their sales activities.

There are a plethora of activities you can track, including phone calls made, contacts with clients, opportunities created, meetings set, meetings conducted, and more. But I've found that when organizations track too many metrics, it dilutes the effectiveness of their accountability processes. At the end of the day, you should only be tracking one or two activity metrics at most.

WHAT SALES ACTIVITIES TO TRACK

When it comes to tracking sales activities, the two most powerful indicators of future sales success are meetings set and opportunities created. Depending on your organization, you should choose which of these metrics makes the most sense—and focus specifically on tracking that. If both metrics apply to your organization, great. If only one seems to fit, that's fine, too.

The two most powerful indicators of future sales success are meetings set and opportunities created.

Do you know how many meetings your salespeople should set each week in order to ultimately hit sales goals? More important, do your salespeople know? Do you know how many opportunities your salespeople should create each month to hit goals? Do your salespeople know? It's incredibly easily to back into these numbers, so don't worry if you have no idea. We'll figure this out together now, using what I call the Prospecting Playbook, so you can start to get your salespeople to think in terms of these core activities:

Prospecting Playbook

A. **What does the salesperson have to earn in order to support his or her personal goals?** Calculate what the total annual pay (bonus + commission + salary) must be: $_____

B. **What does the salesperson have to sell this year in order to earn that much money?** Given the compensation structure, calculate what the salesperson's total annual sales must be to earn what's needed: $_____

This is now the salesperson's PERSONAL annual sales goal. (NOTE: This has nothing to do with quota! This is the salesperson's own number, not a directive.)

C. **How much __NEW__ business does the salesperson have to close in order to hit that annual sales goal?** Presumably, the salesperson will have at least some existing business coming in, so just ballpark the amount that will have to be NEW: $_____

D. **What is the average annual client value, in dollars?** Just ballpark an average sale's revenue for this salesperson: $_____

E. **How many __NEW__ clients does this salesperson need to close this year to hit the personal sales goal?** Divide the annual sales goal by the average sale ([line C] / [line D]): _____

F. **In order to close one new client, how many initial sales meetings does the salesperson need to conduct?** This is obviously going to be an estimate:

_____

G. **How many sales meetings must the salesperson set this year in order to hit the goal?** Multiply the number of new clients needed to close this year by the number of meetings the salesperson needs in order to close one new client ([line E] x [line F]):

_____

H. How many sales meetings must the salesperson set per week in order to hit the goal? Divide the number of sales meetings the salesperson must set this year by 50 ([line G] / 50]): _____

This salesperson must set _____ meetings per week in order to achieve his or her personal goal.

 *You can download a free PDF version of this template in my Key Pages & Worksheets Guide at www.MarcWayshak.com/HighVelocity.*

Let's say Susan has a personal annual sales goal of $2 million. She already has an existing book of $1 million, so she will have to close $1 million in new business. The average sale size at her organization is $100,000. This means that Susan needs to close approximately 10 new pieces of business in order to hit her sales goal.

Now that you know Susan needs to close 10 new pieces of business a year, it's time to figure out how many discovery meetings she needs to set, on average, in order to close one new piece of business. The average close ratio for new business across the sales organization is 20%, from initial meeting to closed sale. That means Susan needs to set five discovery meetings in order to close one new sale.

So, Susan must set 50 discovery meetings over the course of the year in order to close $1 million in new business and ultimately be on track to hit her sales goal of $2 million. More simply, Susan has to set one discovery meeting with a new prospect each week in order to be on track to hit her numbers.

Now, go through the above scenario using actual numbers from your sales team, plugging in the key metric that makes the most sense for your organization. This is where you start to make a customized plan for each salesperson. You need to lay out a plan for each salesperson individually. Once the plan is there, and the information is being entered into the CRM system, this process will enable management to measure the right sales activities while formalizing a prospecting cadence for the entire team.

As you've seen many times already in this book, success in sales is a very simple math formula. If your salespeople do the right activities correctly, with the right level of frequency, then they will hit or exceed their sales goals.

The question is, are you actually measuring those activities? If the answer is no, then that's something you absolutely must change. The most basic levels of sales infrastructure require that you measure your salespeople's activities. Failure to do so will create huge confusion within your sales team.

You need to lay out a plan for each salesperson individually.

Measurements clarify the expectations of your sales team and provide structure for your salespeople. In particular, the number of sales meetings set by your team is a powerful metric to track. According to my research, meetings are such a key metric for top performers that they're more than twice as likely than non-top performers to complain that they're wasting time driving to meetings.[125]

Here's an example of a manager's dashboard tracking the sales team's meetings:

Meeting Metrics

Sales Meetings Set Last Week by Team:	21
Sales Meetings Set This Week by Team:	23
Sales Meetings That Occured Last Week	27
Sales Meetings Occuring This Week:	18

Meetings Set This Week

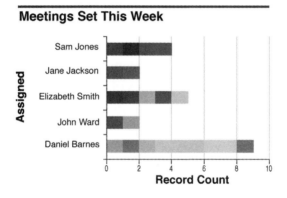

Meetings Scheduled by Rep- Current & Next Month

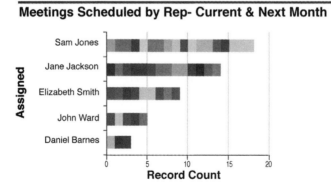

Your salespeople need to know, with the utmost level of clarity, exactly what they need to do on a daily, weekly, and monthly basis in order to hit their numbers. If they don't, then there will be a severe disconnect between day-to-day activities and sales goals.

TRACKING SALES PIPELINES

Now that we've covered tracking sales activities, it's time to dive into tracking the other leading indicator of sales success: sales pipeline opportunities. By looking at the sales pipeline today, we can accurately forecast what salespeople will be selling a month, a quarter, or even a year from now.

While many organizations track sales pipelines in some way, they rarely measure the most effective metrics. The most common mistake I see is that sales organizations view the pipeline as a sort of snapshot of all the deals that are currently in play. With this approach, they miss a golden opportunity to use the pipeline as a way to forecast sales into the future.

By looking at the sales pipeline today, we can accurately forecast what salespeople will be selling a month, a quarter, or even a year from now.

What typically happens is that a manager with good intentions will initiate a "pipeline review" with a salesperson. Very quickly, though, these pipeline reviews turn into deal reviews. The manager goes through the pipeline, asks about a specific deal—and then the conversation turns into a talk about that specific deal. The manager and salesperson end up going through each of the deals in the pipeline, getting stuck in the weeds on each one. The tangent has become the focus.

A true pipeline review—the kind your sales management should be conducting—focuses exclusively on the actual health of the pipeline. To that end, there are four main components of any successful pipeline review:

1. Volume.

Is the volume of the pipeline where it needs to be? This is a critical question to answer. Volume is measured by the overall weighted value of the pipeline. In a healthy pipeline, the weighted value of the pipeline is at least equal to the salesperson's goal during a typical sales cycle. Weighted value of an opportunity is the overall potential value of a sale multiplied by *the percentage of the likelihood* to close that sale in a given moment.

I know that's an earful, so let me explain. Let's say a salesperson has an opportunity with a potential value of $100,000. The opportunity is currently in the presentation phase, so we might give it a 50% likelihood of closing after we determine that it's highly qualified. So, in order to get the weighted value of that opportunity, we simply multiply the potential value of the sale ($100,000) by the likelihood that it will close (50%). The weighted value of that single opportunity is $50,000. The weighted value of the *overall pipeline* is the sum of all the individual weighted values of each opportunity.

Volume is measured by the overall weighted value of the pipeline.

Managers and salespeople often push back on the validity of a pipeline's weighted value. They say, "It doesn't make sense: Just because a $100,000 opportunity has a 50% likelihood of closing, that doesn't mean it's actually worth $50,000." While this is true about each opportunity individually, the math works when we take all the opportunities together for a combined weighted value. Why? Because everything tends to average out. Salespeople lose one sale; they win another.

In the end, a pipeline's weighted value can be a strong indicator of health, provided that the salesperson is using an effective sales process and thus has real insight into the sale.

> *A pipeline's weighted value can be a strong indicator of health, provided that the salesperson is using an effective sales process.*

Weighted value is particularly effective for pipelines with 20 opportunities or more. Of course, if a salesperson has a pipeline with only three opportunities, then weighted value won't be a good way to predict success. But if there are only three opportunities, then it's nearly impossible to forecast sales anyway—there's simply too much volatility.

By focusing on weighted value during a pipeline review, sales managers can quickly understand whether a salesperson is actually on track to hit numbers. If the weighted value is equal to or greater than the salesperson's goal for a given sales cycle, then the salesperson is in good shape. If it's less, then the salesperson is in trouble, and it's time to increase sales activities to get more opportunities into that pipeline.

2. New opportunities.

Does the salesperson have new opportunities consistently coming into the pipeline? Or are there a lot of older deals? During pipeline reviews, your sales managers should keep track of how many new opportunities are actually entering the pipeline on a weekly or monthly basis.

Sales activity is the blood that pumps through the veins of the sales pipeline.

3. Velocity.

Is the pipeline's velocity appropriate? When it comes to sales cycle length, we all know there can be a range. But in order to answer this question about velocity, you need to determine the typical sales cycle at your company. It could be one week, three months, six months, or a year—it totally depends on your organization.

Whatever it is, notice the velocity with which opportunities cycle through the pipeline in relation to the typical sales cycle. Are opportunities stalling in the pipeline, or are they moving along at an appropriate pace for what's typical in your industry?

During pipeline reviews, if a manager notices that velocity is slower than it should be, one of the best metrics to measure is the last time the opportunity was updated in the CRM. Create a column in the pipeline report that shows the date when the opportunity was last updated. If it's been a month or two, that's a problem. Whether it's a data entry issue or a sales activity issue, the manager will have a sense of how to proceed to help the salesperson increase velocity.

4. Next steps.

Does every opportunity have a clear and scheduled next step? Failing to establish a next step is the kiss of death for sales. When the category for "next steps" is blank, that's a red flag during a pipeline review. Every single opportunity should show a clear and scheduled next step. This is extremely easy to track and one of the most important factors during a pipeline review. Here's an example of a good basic sales pipeline report:

Opp Report Trimmed

Summarize information by:	Date Field	Range
Opportunity Owner	Close Date	Custom

Show	Opportunity Status	Probability
All opportunities	Open	All

Run Report	Hide Details	Customize	Save	Save As	Delete	Printable View	Export Details

Grouped By: Opportunity Owner
Sorted By: Opportunity Owner

Probability (%)	Stage	Account Name	Opportunity Name	Age	Last Activity	Close Date	Next Step	Amount	Expected Revenue
Opportunity Owner: Jim Newton (43 records)				avg 267,907				USD 2,988,614.50	USD 1,057,436.15
60%	Solution	ATD Widgets	EDPA Analysis	259	2/6/2018	2/16/2018	meeting with Joe in Janurary- will follow up ahead of time	USD 40,000.00	USD 24,000.00
30%	Qualification	Smith Co	RAD Change Order	437	12/21/2017	2/15/2018	Meeting with Samatha in DC in Janurary	USD 25,000.00	USD 7,500.00
30%	Qualification	Wexler & Winehart	DME-OMT Development	259	1/1/2018	2/16/2018	schedule call for end of January	USD 10,900.00	USD 3,270.00
30%	Qualification	St. Marys Hospital	PIOT Project Development	480	1/22/2018	2/15/2018	lunch meeting at Smoke on the Water in February with Tom and Dirk	USD 50,000.00	USD 15,000.00
96%	Contact	LM Inc.	DEX Development	17	1/20/2018	2/28/2018	Meeting at LM on 2/3 with Rocco and Melissa	USD 567.00	USD 538.65
30%	Qualification	Handcock Funds	WBDT protfolio case	315	12/18/2017	2/28/2018	Follow up after tax season is over	USD 25,000.00	USD 7,500.00
30%	Qualification	Raleigh Flooring	ROD Migration	301	8/25/2017	2/28/2018	Scheduled meeting with Bethany Smith	USD 20,000.00	USD 6,000.00
25%	Qualification	Johnson LTD	TAM Analysis	543	10/18/2017	2/28/2018	Kick off meeting planned for 1/15 with Rockwell Howard	USD 250,000.00	USD 62,500.00
50%	Solution	K&M Supply	MM Supply Leadership	543	11/23/2017	2/28/2018	Conference call with team planned for early February- date to be confirmed	USD 197,720.00	USD 97,860.00

Using the Sales Process to Track Opportunities

In addition to pipeline reviews that include the four main components listed above, a highly effective pipeline system will also use the sales process itself to track opportunities. What I mean by that is, every step of your sales process should have its own dedicated field in the CRM for each individual opportunity. Any marginally sophisticated sales organization should make these minor customizations to the CRM opportunity fields.

I always have my clients add the disqualification CUPBAN steps directly into the opportunity pipeline. Therefore, all thorough opportunities will have information about key challenges, financial upside, personal motivations for the prospect, budget, authority in the decision-making process, and next steps.

The next steps field is arguably the single most important field in an opportunity, because next steps are what drive all pipeline progress. That's why we began this section talking about sales activity. Sales activity is the blood that pumps through the veins of the sales pipeline.

Far too often, when managers notice that pipeline volume isn't as high as it should be, they consider it a pipeline problem. But it's not. It's a sales activity problem. The same is true for pipeline velocity: The speed at which opportunities move through the sales cycle isn't a pipeline problem. It's a sales strategy problem. This means that, on the front lines in the field, your salespeople aren't using an effective sales strategy to get opportunities through the pipeline.

Here's an example of a pipeline visual in a manager's dashboard:

Sales Pipeline - A Accounts

$32,143.83

$102,482.00

$312,426.70

$15,283.25

Sum of Expected Revenue in USD

Stage

■ Discovery   Qualification   ■ Proposed   ■Contract

In fact, pipeline issues are always sales strategy or activity issues, not actual pipeline issues. We fix pipeline issues by changing something about strategy or activity, not the pipeline itself.

Remember that the health of the sales pipeline is a leading indicator of whether a salesperson is on track to hit goals. But it's only an indicator of the effectiveness of that person's sales strategy and sales activities—not an indicator of that person's success at actually putting information in the pipeline report. That's something you need to enforce.

In fact, there are two questions you need to answer before you can track any opportunities in the CRM effectively:

1. How are you ensuring that the right information is going into the system?

2. How are you ensuring that you're pulling the right information out of the system?

GETTING THE RIGHT DATA INTO THE SYSTEM

The trickier of the two questions is the first. Ensuring that the right data gets into the system can be a huge challenge for sales organizations. One of the biggest roadblocks is that many salespeople don't track their interactions with clients and prospects in the CRM. This has to change.

When a salesperson has a call with a client, that call must be entered into the system. While your salespeople might be tracking calls some other way—such as in a spreadsheet or in a notebook—those workaround systems have got to stop.

There are a few tools out there that can help your salespeople more easily enter information into the CRM. The first is email integration, which allows salespeople to simply use their Outlook or Google email platforms to automatically enter information directly into the CRM. This includes calendar information, email interactions and, in some cases, phone calls. Since most salespeople use their email platforms on a minute-by-minute basis during the selling day, this is incredibly effective.

Ensuring that the right data gets into the system can be a huge challenge for sales organizations.

There are also several phone integration tools that can help your salespeople more quickly and accurately enter call information into the CRM. Instead of manually dialing and then logging every call into the system, your salespeople can just click on a contact's name or phone number to auto-dial the prospect, and an end-of-call prompt will enable them to enter the information from the call directly into the CRM. This makes phone calls much easier to track.

Keep in mind that many CRM systems are savvy about these data-entry issues, and they already integrate with tools that salespeople tend to use on a daily basis. So, depending on your CRM, you may not need further integration tools to achieve a system that helps your salespeople automatically enter the right information.

PULLING THE RIGHT DATA OUT OF THE SYSTEM

This is simple. As long as the right information is going into the CRM, it's easy to put together activity reports that track meetings set, emails sent, calls made, and opportunities created.

Once you've identified the key metrics you want to measure—meetings set, for example—you'll create a dashboard report that tracks meetings set for the past week for each salesperson. This will give you a quick snapshot of what each salesperson has done over the course of each week.

If a manager sees that a salesperson has only set one meeting when the expectation was to set five, the manager can intervene and coach accordingly. On the other hand, if a salesperson is consistently exceeding meeting numbers but still isn't hitting sales goals, then the manager will know that something is going wrong during those sales meetings.

This data gives powerful insight into measuring what salespeople are doing. Every CRM system has easy ways to measure these basic activities. The far greater challenge, as we discussed earlier, is making sure the information is going in correctly in the first place.

Chapter 10:

Team Meetings & Coaching

NOW THAT WE'VE laid out the sales accountability process, we tie all of it together with two major components of sales management: sales team meetings and sales coaching. These are two essentially independent parts of sales management. Sales team meetings focus on the overall big-picture accountability of what salespeople are doing on a weekly or monthly basis, whereas sales coaching focuses on specific tactics and development in a 1:1 relationship between manager and salesperson.

We'll start with sales team meetings, since they're one of the biggest weaknesses at organizations. Most sales team meetings are a massive waste of time. If you conducted an anonymous poll today asking your salespeople about the effectiveness of their team meetings, it's highly unlikely that it would bring back positive news.

SALES TEAM MEETINGS

Most organizations either run weak sales team meetings or they don't run any sales team meetings at all. When it comes to gauging the strength of your own sales team meetings, there are two variables to assess: purposefulness and efficiency. The goal is to make sure that these meetings are respectful of your salespeople's time. In order for that to be the case, sales team meetings must be both highly purposeful and highly efficient:

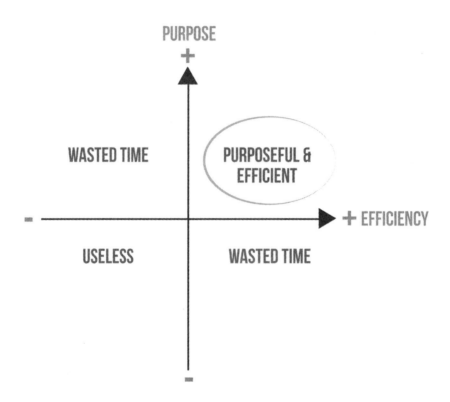

If sales team meetings haven't been successful at your organization yet, it's not because sales team meetings aren't effective in general. It's because your organization isn't doing them right. In this section, I'll lay out exactly what sales team meeting structure you should implement at your organization to dramatically improve their productivity and value.

The single most important rule for purposeful, efficient team meetings is that they must be conducted on a consistent schedule. Human beings thrive in structure. Organizations that occasionally set sales team meetings, or haphazardly schedule them throughout the year, create chaos and frustration in the lives of their salespeople. Any high-velocity sales organization will have a consistent cadence as to when team meetings are conducted.

Most organizations should be conducting weekly sales team meetings at the same time on the same exact day every week. If that's impossible for your organization, once every two weeks or once a month is acceptable. But when you start conducting team meetings less than once a month, you're missing out on a lot of the structure and value of these meetings.

The next critical component is a strict agenda. In just a minute, you're going to read a sample agenda that lays out the specific elements that should be covered in sales team meetings, as well as specific periods of time that should be allotted to each element. Be vigilant about adhering to these set timeframes and your sales managers will show

> *The single most important rule for purposeful, efficient team meetings is that they must be conducted on a consistent schedule.*

a high degree of respect for salespeople's time. There's nothing worse for salespeople than when a meeting that was supposed to be 45 minutes turns into nearly two hours, just because the manager in charge is weak at time management. People who run purposeful, efficient meetings are militant about sticking to the allotted time slots for each item on the agenda.

The final factor I want to mention is group size. The most successful team meetings include a group of six salespeople or fewer. If you have 12 people on your sales team, that means you should break up team meetings into two separate groups. Maybe one meeting includes the six top performers on the team, and the other meeting includes the bottom performers. You can also break the meetings up by region. Whatever you do, don't conduct sales team meetings with more than six salespeople in the room. It's simply too big a group to cover everything.

The most successful team meetings include a group of six salespeople or fewer.

Now, let's jump right into the ideal sales team meeting agenda. The agenda below assumes a group of five salespeople attending weekly sales team meetings:

1. **Commitment reviews (5 minutes total – 1 minute/ person)**

   Reviewing commitments is one of the backbones of purposeful sales meetings. Any effective meeting will inspire action. If no action comes out of the meeting, it's a waste of time.

   Commitments are core drivers of sales activity. They're also the glue that connects this week's team meeting to next week's. Sales team meetings should begin with a review of each salesperson's commitments from the previous week. Have those commitments been fulfilled? If not, why? These are the key questions to answer for each salesperson.

One minute should be allotted for each salesperson to review commitments, and the manager should personally check to make sure that each commitment was completed. It's important to note that a commitment must be something that salespeople can say they specifically did or did not do. "Make more dials this week" is not a commitment. "Make 35 dials this week" is. The more specific, the better.

If no action comes out of the meeting, it's a waste of time.

What's more, salespeople must have direct control over performing and completing the task. That's why "close the deal with XYZ Company" isn't an acceptable commitment, but "set a meeting with my contact at XYZ Company" is.

2. Pipeline reviews (15 minutes – 3 minutes/person)

As we discussed in the last chapter, pipeline reviews are not the same as deal reviews. Sales meeting pipeline reviews focus on the new activity in the pipeline, what's been updated recently, and any other developments that have been added, such as new opportunities and next steps. It's not about getting into the minutia of specific deals. Spending three minutes on each salesperson, the manager in charge should look at the overall weighted value of the team's pipelines to determine health.

3. Key activity reviews (5 minutes – 1 minute/person)

Depending on what metric you've chosen to track and measure, this part of the sales team meeting will focus on a key activity that your salespeople should be doing every week. For example, if you're measuring the number of meetings set per week, then each salesperson will review the number of meetings they set in the past week.

The most effective way to do this is to actually show each salesperson's numbers to the group. This generates competition among the team. If someone only set one sales meeting last week when the goal was five, that person should feel pressure to increase sales activity both from the manager and also from the other salespeople in the room.

4. What's new to share with prospects (5 minutes)

Whoever's leading the sales team meeting should consistently provide salespeople with new tools to use when selling. It requires discipline on the part of the organization to have a steady stream of these tools available.

One example might be a new piece of content from marketing that salespeople can send out to their clients and prospects. Getting into a weekly routine of sharing new tools with prospects will arm them with valuable ways to connect with both potential clients and existing ones. It also puts pressure on marketing to provide sales with the resources they need to generate new leads.

5. Sales training (10 minutes)

Sales training is a critical component of any effective team meeting. When most people think of sales training, they think of a three-day intensive workshop. In reality, people learn much more effectively when they're given small pieces of information at a time, so they can apply and implement new ideas as they go. Research shows that bite-size learning can increase information transfer by 17%—and results in greater understanding, application, and retention than a day-long equivalent.[126]

Sales training is a critical component of any effective team meeting.

Sales training in team meetings should be quick, simple, and consistent. A best practice is to show salespeople a short training video in each meeting that will spark conversation or even a role play. Then, salespeople can go out and use the strategies they learned. On my YouTube channel (www.YouTube.com/MarcWayshak) I have hundreds of videos your managers can use in sales team meetings just for this purpose.

6. Commitments for this week (5 minutes - 1 minute/ person)

These are the commitments salespeople make in the current sales meeting, to be reviewed in the next. Remember, salespeople must have total control over accomplishing the commitments they choose, and they must have the ability to say whether the commitments were fulfilled or not.

"Trying harder this week" is not a commitment. Neither is "closing three sales." Instead, salespeople should choose commitments like: "Ask for five introductions this week. Send out emails to all 50 trade show leads. Make 30 phone calls to prospects." These are all specific, measurable commitments that salespeople have 100% control over. The team will then review these commitments at the start of the next sales team meeting.

 You can download a free PDF version of this meeting agenda in my Key Pages & Worksheets Guide at www.MarcWayshak.com/HighVelocity.

As you can see, there's nothing fancy about a highly purposeful, efficient sales team meeting. What's special about it is the degree of consistency and structure that the meeting creates. Running this exact meeting agenda every week without fail will have a multiplicative effect on the value that it brings to the sales organization, holding salespeople accountable to themselves and to each other.

SALES COACHING

While sales team meetings are all about holding salespeople's feet to the fire to ensure they do what they say they're going to do, coaching is different. While there may be commitments to next steps, sales coaching is really about developing talent and providing salespeople with tools and skills that make them more effective at their jobs.

People often use the terms "coaching" and "training" to mean the same thing, but they're completely different. Training involves *teaching* a particular technique or skill to salespeople. With training, the trainer starts with an answer. If the trainer wants a salesperson to learn a new technique for phone sales, then the training will focus on teaching that specific skill in a directive way.

Coaching, on the other hand, doesn't start with an answer. There's no set idea for what the salesperson should learn, or what needs to be taught. Instead, it's about the coach observing, questioning, and challenging the salesperson in ways that support growth and productivity. If sales training is a monologue, then sales coaching is a dynamic conversation. This type of dynamic yet formal approach to sales coaching has been shown to improve quota attainment by up to 61%.[127]

At the end of this chapter, I'll give you a few brief notes on the best strategies for effective sales training. But since coaching is so much more important to your sales infrastructure, that's what we're going to focus on here.

DIRECTIVE VS. NON-DIRECTIVE COACHING

There are two main types of sales coaching: directive and non-directive. Both types require that the coach first observes selling behavior, watching the salesperson in action. After that, the two approaches diverge. With directive coaching, coaches tell salespeople specifically what they should do differently after observing them in a selling situation. With non-directive coaching, coaches take the approach of asking thoughtful questions of salespeople in order to bring them to their own conclusions about how to improve.

A dynamic yet formal approach to sales coaching has been shown to improve quota attainment by up to 61%.

Most managers rely exclusively on directive coaching. They're in the habit of simply saying what they're thinking, and telling salespeople exactly what to do, right off the bat. The weakness of this strategy is that salespeople are far less likely to implement the ideas, since they didn't come to any conclusions on their own. This is why the best sales coaches are masters of non-directive coaching.

Great coaches ask great questions. Those questions lead salespeople to a certain answer on their own. At the end of the day, good coaching is just about using the sales process on salespeople themselves. It's about good selling. Just like we tell salespeople to ask great questions of their prospects, any good coach will ask great questions of their salespeople.

Below is a list of the top nine questions your sales managers can ask when coaching salespeople:

1. Why?...Why?...Why?

2. Unpack that for me…

3. On a scale of 1 to 10, how would you rate that?

4. What do you think went well with...?

5. What could you have done differently...?

6. What are three takeaways you have from this?

7. What can you put into action this week as a result of this?

8. What are three commitments you will make over the next week?

9. What next steps should we schedule as a result of this?

You can download a free PDF version of these questions in my Key Pages & Worksheets Guide at www.MarcWayshak.com/HighVelocity.

THE RULE OF THREE

The truth is, non-directive coaching doesn't come naturally to most people. That's why I've developed a simple strategy called the Rule of Three. It's easy: In any coaching situation, the coach should ask at least three questions before making a declarative statement. Those three questions should be open-ended, enabling the coach to drill down deep into the salesperson's own thoughts and opinions.

Here's a play-by-play example of the Rule of Three in action:

A manager and a salesperson go into a sales meeting. The salesperson leads the interaction and independently runs the meeting. At the end of the meeting, the salesperson forgets to schedule a next step with the prospect. The manager and salesperson are now debriefing on how the sales meeting went:

Manager: "What do you think could have been different about that meeting?"

Salesperson: "I'm not sure. I think maybe I could have asked more questions."

Manager: "That's fair. But what are three specific changes you could have made about that meeting?"

Salesperson: "I could have asked several more questions, I could have taken better notes, and I could have had a better answer for the prospect's question about the key benefits package."

Manager: "All three of those are great insights. Now, what's the next step with this prospect?"

Salesperson: "Well, I guess I'll check in with her next week."

Manager: "If you were to go back into that meeting, what would you do differently to ensure that there was a clear next step?"

Salesperson: "I would go back and schedule a presentation meeting with a specific time and date. That would have given us a clearer next step."

Manager: "Great idea. Would it be possible to still do that?"

The purpose of the Rule of Three is to get salespeople to learn how to think like problem solvers. It's not about the manager just handing out the answers, even if the salesperson struggles for a while to come to the right conclusion. This approach helps salespeople build the necessary skills to solve problems on their own, rather than depending on the help of a coach to get the answer.

In this way, the best managers use coaching to empower salespeople to become better and more effective than they are. It's a fallacy that the manager has to be the best salesperson. The manager simply has to be the best manager. Great managers often make salespeople better than they are—and that's what effective coaching is all about.

By asking thought-provoking, open-ended questions, your managers won't just lead salespeople to the right answer. They'll also gain a deeper understanding of what really drives your salespeople. This is key.

Understanding each salesperson's "why"—on a 1:1 basis— is critical for coaches to make the most impact. Every salesperson has a reason they pick up the phone every day. It's very rarely about professional success. The reason they want to make more commission isn't usually about career growth. It's about being able to provide for their family, or to create personal wealth, or to be able to afford that condo. Whatever it is, understanding the "why" enables coaches to get inside a salesperson's head for far more effective sales coaching.

Few managers really know why their salespeople want to be successful. Your managers need to find out.

COACHING CADENCE

So, how often should coaching happen? There's no hard answer. At the very least, though, your sales managers should spend one day a month with each salesperson they coach. That day should be spent outside the office, in the field, observing the salesperson selling. Your managers can accompany outside sales reps to meetings with prospects, and shadow inside sales reps as they sell. Commit your managers to a certain number of rep-hours per month. A structure I like to use is eight rep-hours per month with each direct report.

> *Your sales managers should spend one day a month with each salesperson they coach.*

Consistent, 1:1, face-to-face monthly coaching is one of the most powerful differences between high-velocity sales organizations and under-performing ones. Organizations must let go of the idea that sales managers should be mining information in the CRM all the time, answering hundreds of emails every day. When I see this, I think, "This is a manager who doesn't have priorities straight." Instead, have your systems in place so that managers can spend time actually observing salespeople's behavior, and coaching them to improve. Just like the best salespeople spend the majority of their time 1:1 with prospects and clients, the best managers should have the same mentality when it comes to coaching their direct reports.

At the end of the day, coaching is one of the highest ROI activities that your sales management team can implement. That said, it can be a challenge for many managers to embrace coaching in a natural way that doesn't feel forced. Here are my best practices for helping sales management create powerful coaching moments, with relatively low time investment, in organic ways:

1. **Record salespeople's phone calls.**

   With today's technology, it's easy to record sales calls. Even if you have legal concerns about recording prospects or clients, you can still record sales calls by only recording the salesperson's voice. This can be done simply by putting an iPhone or another recording device on the salesperson's desk. However, the best approach is obviously to record both sides of the phone call.

   Gong.io is a game-changing tool that can be plugged in to record every sales call your salespeople make, which will then pick up on key traits like listening-to-talking ratio and number of questions asked. Have your sales managers review these recorded calls with each salesperson individually, and then develop specific data around each salesperson's strengths and weaknesses on the phone.

This data can give your managers valuable insight into what salespeople are doing right—and wrong—during the sales process. Research shows that only 37% of salespeople are consistently effective on the phone, while 63% of salespeople conduct behavior on the phone that actually drives down overall sales performance.[128]

2. **Sit in the sales bullpen.**

If you have salespeople working in the office, then your sales managers should spend a certain number of hours each month just sitting in the sales bullpen, listening and observing. Even the CEO can do this. This approach is a great way to encourage off-the-cuff coaching moments with salespeople.

> *Only 37% of salespeople are consistently effective on the phone, while 63% of salespeople conduct behavior on the phone that actually drives down overall sales performance.*

3. **Conduct coaching meetings.**

Every manager should have a weekly 30-minute to hour-long coaching meeting with each direct report. There are three key components that will make these coaching meetings effective:

1. **Meeting prep**: The manager should review the CRM prior to each meeting.

2. **Agenda**: Each coaching meeting should have a specific plan to follow.

3. **Meeting debrief**: The manager and salesperson should create at least three tactical takeaways or next steps at the end of each coaching meeting.

4. **Use Monday Morning Quarterback hot seats.**

These hot seats are one of my all-time favorite coaching techniques. On a consistent schedule, one salesperson is put in the "hot seat" during a sales team meeting. That salesperson fills out a form that lays out his or her particular process for a prospect, including where the deal currently is in the sales cycle, what's known about the prospect, and any scheduled next steps. From there, the rest of the sales team dissects the salesperson's process, asking questions and digging into the details of the deal.

The power of this activity is that it gets the whole team to participate in the coaching process. They start to think like coaches themselves. It's important for salespeople to have practice looking at opportunities other than their own, so they can apply the sales process as an outsider, without the pressure of making a sale. Below is the Monday Morning Quarterback form that I use. Feel free to copy it and distribute it to your team during your next sales team meeting:

MONDAY MORNING QUARTERBACK

1. What are you trying to sell?_____

2. What is the sale worth to you? _____

---

3. How did you originally find this prospect?
Cold call_____ Referral_____ Existing Client_____
Client Introduction_____
Other: _____

4. Have you ever sold this prospect anything? ___
What? _____

5. How long have you been working on this
opportunity? _____

6. Who else have you taken on a call with you?
Another salesperson_____
Technical support _____
Management _____
Other _____

7. How many contacts have you had with this pros-
pect (for this opportunity)?
Telephone_____ Face-to-face _____ Letter _____
E-mail _____
Other _____

8. With whom have you met?
Name _____
Title _____
Name _____
Title _____
Name _____
Title _____

9. Have these been 1:1 meetings, group
meetings, a combination? _____
Please explain the meeting dynamics:

_____

10. Where are you in the sales process?
    Challenge 1: _____
    Challenge 2: _____
    Challenge 3: _____
    Value of Upside: _____
    Personal Stake:_____
    Budget: _____
    Authority Process:
    Who: _____
    What: _____
    When: _____
    How: _____
    Where: _____
    Why: _____
    Anyone Else: _____
    Presentation? _____
    Demonstration: Yes/No
    Who actually attended or will attend?_____
    _____
    First referral and introduction meeting date:
    _____

11. Do you have an Org Chart? _____

12. Who is your champion? _____

13. What are the next steps?_____

14. Scale of 1 to 10 chance of this deal closing?
    _____

15. What have you learned from this exercise?
    _____

Other Notes:

_____

_____

_____

_____

You can download a free PDF version of this template in my Key Pages & Worksheets Guide at www.MarcWayshak.com/HighVelocity.

A NOTE ON SALES TRAINING...

There are two parts of sales training that I want to cover:

1. Initial training.

The initial training teaches your salespeople the new sales process your company is adopting. Every salesperson should have a systematic sales process to follow—and that process should be the same for everyone on the sales team. For example, the sales process I've shared with you in this book should be introduced to the team through training. It might take a series of trainings—perhaps one or two days over the course of a couple of quarters—to teach the nuts and bolts of the system.

2. Reinforcement.

Reinforcing the ideas from sales training depends on your sales management team. This, in many ways, is even more important than the initial training itself: High-performing sales organizations are twice as likely to provide ongoing training to the sales team as low-performing ones.[129]

Create a regular cadence of training reinforcement sessions, ideally at least once per week in sales team meetings. There can also be ongoing sales training outside of sales team meetings, but the point is that management reinforces the new sales process through multiple channels in your sales infrastructure. You can use my YouTube videos as trainings to achieve consistent reinforcement of the sales process outlined in this book.

Closing Thoughts

IN 1958, THE Green Bay Packers were one of the worst teams in the NFL. Even though they had five future Hall-of-Famers playing on their team, they finished with a record of 1-10-1. This was the worst finishing record in team history. The players were distraught and demoralized. The shareholders were discouraged. And the Green Bay community had all but given up on the team.

In fact, things were so bad that the financial viability of the Green Bay Packers was called into question. People were unsure whether the team should even exist anymore. The head coach at the time, Scooter Maclean, was known for never enforcing his own rules. He allowed general chaos to rule the team instead. The future of the Packers was so dim that players were regularly quitting right in the middle of games.

Then, on February 2, 1959, a relatively unknown coach named Vince Lombardi accepted the position of head coach for the Green Bay Packers—and everything transformed.

Lombardi instituted a level of discipline previously unthinkable for most players on the team. Between grueling training regimens and exceptionally high expectations of players' commitment, change became inevitable.

The team's 1959 season finished with a strong 7-5 record. The transformation was so impressive that Lombardi won the award for NFL's Coach of the Year. This was the precursor to one of the greatest coaching careers of all time. Despite a career cut very short by his untimely death, Lombardi is almost universally agreed-upon by experts as the greatest football coach ever, winning nearly 75% of all the games he coached in the NFL.

Looking at your own sales organization today, you may or may not have as heavy a lift as Vince Lombardi did coming into that '58 Packers team. Yet the experience is still instructive for all of us.

Lombardi came in with a clear plan. First, he knew he had to replace those players who were simply unwilling to work within his system—and he had to replace them with top performers. Next, he had to introduce a new strategy to more consistently win games. And finally, he had to implement a management style that expected total commitment from his players, yet also rewarded them for greatness.

As you look to build your own high-velocity sales organization, you must also raise the bar for your team.

As you look to build your own high-velocity sales organization, you must also raise the bar for your team. That means recruiting and retaining top performers. That means instituting a strong sales strategy that's intentional, consistent, and helps your people stand out in the marketplace. And that means building a sales infrastructure that holds your team accountable, yet also gets out of the way— so that your salespeople can do what they have to do to achieve their own personal goals.

These types of changes don't happen overnight. They take time. They take commitment. They require a disciplined approach. But when thoughtfully implemented, these changes can make a massive impact on your top and bottom lines.

Now is action time.

Over 100 times a year, I ask audiences, "What do you think separates the winners from the losers?" Inevitably people shout out terms like "perseverance," "passion," and "enthusiasm"—none of these are wrong, but they miss the key point. Ultimately, the biggest differentiator between those who will remain stuck in mediocrity and those who will grow and thrive is simply *action*. It's about implementing the right ideas, right now.

So what action will you take? What are the two or three ideas you're committed to implementing as a result of reading this book? Albert Einstein once famously said, "Nothing happens until something moves."

What do you intend to make move as a result of the ideas in this book?

How Marc Can Help You

Marc serves as a trusted advisor to help organizations develop the strategy to create massive sales growth. Specifically, he helps clients:

- Simplify sales leadership structure
- Align sales incentives
- Hire world-class sales talent
- Increase close ratios of sales teams
- Increase prospecting output
- Increase top-line revenue

Marc commonly helps clients achieve the following objectives:

- Developing a systematic process for closing sales
- Creating prospecting consistency to increase the output of the sales team
- Establishing a clear sales management strategy to support the sales team
- Rolling out a hiring process that attracts only A players
- Refining existing sales processes to accelerate sales growth
- Developing specific sales activity metrics for each salesperson
- Improving pipeline planning and reporting for the sales team
- Implementing sales management systems to lay foundation for a larger sales team

Marc's highest-impact consulting option is his Sales CEO Advisory Board. To learn how you can join, visit **www.MarcWayshak.com/SalesCEOAdvisory** for more information.

Endnotes

INTRODUCTION:

1   R "Ray" Wang, "Constellation's 2014 Outlook on Dominating Digital Business Disruption: Making Sense of the Digital Business Disruption Trends Through the Lens of a Futurist Framework," Constellation Research, February 10, 2014.

2   Mark J. Perry, "Fortune 500 firms 1955 v. 2017: Only 60 remain, thanks to the creative destruction that fuels economic prosperity," AEI.org, October 20, 2017. See http://www.aei.org/publication/fortune-500-firms-1955-v-2017-only-12-remain-thanks-to-the-creative-destruction-that-fuels-economic-prosperity.

3   Steve Denning, "Why Did IBM Survive?" Forbes.com, July 10, 2011. See https://www.forbes.com/sites/stevedenning/2011/07/10/why-did-ibm-survive.

4   Chris Orlob, "The VP Sales' Job Tenure Has Shrunk 7 Months—This Trend Explains Why," Gong.io, January 29, 2018. See https://www.gong.io/blog/vp-sales-average-tenure/

5   CSO Insights, "Running Up the Down Escalator: 2017 CSO Insights World-Class Sales Practices Report," CSOinsights.com, 2017. See https://www.csoinsights.com/wp-content/uploads/sites/5/2017/08/2017-World-Class-Sales-Practices-Report.pdf

6   Thor Olavsrud, "6 Analytics Trends That Will Shape Business In 2016," CIO.com, January 25, 2016. See https://www.cio.com/article/3025869/analytics/6-analytics-trends-that-will-shape-business-in-2016.html.

7   United States Bureau of Labor Statistics, "Employed and unemployed persons by occupation, not seasonally adjusted," www.bls.gov, 2018. See https://www.bls.gov/news.release/empsit.t13.html.

8   Career Builder, "44 Percent of Employers Plan to Hire in the New Year, According to CareerBuilder's Annual Forecast," www.CareerBuilder.com, 2018. See http://press.careerbuilder.com/2018-01-09-44-Percent-of-Employers-Plan-to-Hire-in-the-New-Year-According-to-CareerBuilders-Annual-Forecast.

9   Steve W. Martin, "B2B Buyer Persona Research," Stevewmartin.com, 2017. See http://wp.stevewmartin.com/how-buyers-select-vendors-and-salespeople.

10   Mimi An, "Buyers Speak Out: How Sales Needs to Evolve," HubSpot.com, April 7, 2016. See https://research.hubspot.com/buyers-speak-out-how-sales-needs-to-evolve.

11   Marc Wayshak, "The Salespeople Perceptions 2018 Survey," Marc Wayshak Sales Research & Insights, May 2018. See MarcWayshak.com/Sales-Statistics.

12   Mimi An, "Buyers Speak Out: How Sales Needs to Evolve," HubSpot.com, April 7, 2016. See https://research.hubspot.com/buyers-speak-out-how-sales-needs-to-evolve.

13   Tibi Puiu, "Your smartphone is millions of times more powerful than all of NASA's combined computing in 1969," zmescience.com, September 10, 2017. See https://www.zmescience.com/research/technology/smartphone-power-compared-to-apollo-432.

14   Salesforce, "Second Annual State of Sales Report,"
      2017. See https://a.sfdcstatic.com/content/dam/
      www/ocms/assets/pdf/misc/state-of-sales-report-
      salesforce.pdf.

15   Karla Lant, "By 2020, There Will Be 4 Devices for Every
      Human on Earth," Futurism.com, June 18, 2017. See
      https://futurism.com/by-2020-there-will-be-4-devic-
      es-for-every-human-on-earth.

16   Aja Frost, "75 Mind-Blowing Sales Statistics That
      Will Help You Sell Smarter in 2018," HubSpot.com,
      January 2, 2018. See https://blog.hubspot.com/sales/
      sales-statistics.

17   Mariah Parker, "How The North Face is using Artificial
      Intelligence to close the gap between the in-store
      and online experience," BuzzRobot.com, November
      13, 2017. See https://buzzrobot.com/how-the-north-
      face-is-using-artificial-intelligence-to-close-the-gap-
      between-the-in-store-and-bea464ae0293.

18   Steven W. Martin, "B2B Buyer Persona Research,"
      Stevewmartin.com, 2017. See http://wp.stevewmartin.
      com/how-buyers-select-vendors-and-salespeople.

19   Salesforce, "Second Annual State of Sales Report,"
      2017. See https://a.sfdcstatic.com/content/dam/
      www/ocms/assets/pdf/misc/state-of-sales-report-
      salesforce.pdf.

20   Accenture, "Empowering Your Sales Force: It's Not
      Just Automation. It's Personal," 2016. See https://
      www.accenture.com/t20160408T020032__w__/
      us-en/_acnmedia/PDF-12/Accenture-Empowering-
      Your-Sales-Force-Digital-Sales-Info-Final.pdf.

Section I: Performers

21   Herbert Greenberg, How to Hire and Develop Your Next Top Performer (New York: McGraw Hill, 2001).

22   Harvard Business Review, "How to Predict Turnover on Your Sales Team," HBR. org, 2017. See https://hbr.org/2017/07/how-to-predict-turnover-on-your-sales-team.

23   Herbert Greenberg, How to Hire and Develop Your Next Top Performer (New York: McGraw Hill, 2001).

24   Mimi An, "How Salespeople Learn," HubSpot.com, June 12, 2017. See: https://research.hubspot.com/how-salespeople-learn.

25   Scott Fuhr, "Good Hiring Makes Good Cents," SellingPower.com, August 2, 2012. See https://www.sellingpower.com/2012/08/02/9930/good-hiring-makes-good-cents.

26   Steve W. Martin, "What's Wrong with Salespeople Today," Stevewmartin.com, 2017. See http://wp.stevewmartin.com/buyers-report-whats-wrong-with-salespeople.

27   Gong.io, "Nine Secret Elements of Highly Effective Sales Conversations E-Book," Gong.io, February 5, 2017.

28   CareerBuilder, "More than 1 in 4 Employers Do Not Conduct Background Checks of All New Employees, According to CareerBuilder Survey," CareerBuilder.com, November 17, 2016. See http://www.career-builder.com/share/aboutus/pressreleasesdetail.aspx.

29   Steve W. Martin, "Research on Top Salespeople,
      Sales Leaders and Win-Loss Analysis Studies,"
      Stevewmartin.com, 2017. See http://wp.stevewmartin.
      com/win-loss-research-articles-and-white-papers.

30   Bradford D. Smart and Greg Alexander, Topgrading
      for Sales: World-Class Methods to Interview, Hire,
      and Coach Top Sales Representatives (New York:
      Portfolio/Penguin, 2008), 35.

31   Adam M. Grant, "Rethinking the Extraverted Sales
      Ideal: The Ambivert Advantage," Psychological Science
      24, no. 6 (June 2013): 1024–30. See http://journals.
      sagepub.com/doi/abs/10.1177/0956797612463706.

32   Richard A. Rocco, "2015-2016 Sales Effectiveness—
      Sales Acceleration Survey," DePaul University,
      2016. See: http://8c9afd081c3d4def1403-dc063f7c-
      0c33274a6b24fd15453f7b6d.r25.cf2.rackcdn.com/
      a8f5faff75824f519f277ac34aa53e40.pdf.

33   LinkedIn, "Global Recruiting Trends 2017." See https://
      business.linkedin.com/content/dam/me/business/
      en-us/talent-solutions/resources/pdfs/linkedin-glob-
      al-recruiting-trends-report.pdf.

34   Boris Groysberg, Nitin Nohria and Claudio Fernandez-
      Arao, "The Definitive Guide to Recruiting in Good
      Times and Bad," HBR.org, May, 2009. See https://hbr.
      org/2009/05/the-definitive-guide-to-recruiting-in-
      good-times-and-bad.

35   Scott Fuhr, "Good Hiring Makes Good Cents,"
      SellingPower.com, August 2, 2012. See https://
      www.sellingpower.com/2012/08/02/9930/
      good-hiring-makes-good-cents.

36   LinkedIn, "Global Recruiting Trends 2017." See https://business.linkedin.com/content/dam/me/business/en-us/talent-solutions/resources/pdfs/linkedin-global-recruiting-trends-report.pdf.

37   LinkedIn, "Global Recruiting Trends 2017." See https://business.linkedin.com/content/dam/me/business/en-us/talent-solutions/resources/pdfs/linkedin-global-recruiting-trends-report.pdf.

38   Boris Groysberg, Nitin Nohria and Claudio Fernandez-Arao, "The Definitive Guide to Recruiting in Good Times and Bad," HBR.org, May, 2009. See https://hbr.org/2009/05/the-definitive-guide-to-recruiting-in-good-times-and-bad.

39   Richard A. Rocco, "2015-2016 Sales Effectiveness—Sales Acceleration Survey," DePaul University, 2016. See: http://8c9afd081c3d4def1403-dc063f7c-0c33274a6b24fd15453f7b6d.r25.cf2.rackcdn.com/a8f5faff75824f519f277ac34aa53e40.pdf.

40   Jason Dana, Robyn Dawes and Nathanial Peterson, "Belief in the unstructured interview: The persistence of an illusion," Judgment and Decision Making: 8, 512-520. 2013. See: https://www.researchgate.net/publication/286345463_Belief_in_the_unstructured_interview_The_persistence_of_an_illusion.

41   Frank Schmidt and John E. Hunter. "The Validity and Utility of Selection Methods in Personnel Psychology," Psychological Bulletin: 124, 262-274. 1998. See http://mavweb.mnsu.edu/howard/Schmidt%20and%20Hunter%201998%20Validity%20and%20Utility%20Psychological%20Bulletin.pdf.

42 Alexander Todorov, "First impressions: Making up your mind after a 100-ms exposure to a face," Psychological Science: 7, 592-8. 2006. See: http://journals.sagepub.com/doi/abs/10.1111/j.1467-9280.2006.01750.x.

43 Robert Hogan, Tomas Chamorro-Premuzic, And Robert B. Kaiser, "Employability And Career Success: Bridging The Gap Between Theory And Reality," Industrial And Organizational Psychology, 6 (2013), 3–16.

44 Adam M. Grant, "Rethinking the Extraverted Sales Ideal: The Ambivert Advantage," Psychological Science 24, no. 6 (June 2013): 1024–30. See http://journals.sagepub.com/doi/abs/10.1177/0956797612463706.

45 Jobvite, "Jobvite Recruiter Nation Report," Jobvite.com, 2016. See: http://www.jobvite.com/wp-content/uploads/2016/09/RecruiterNation2016.pdf.

46 Bridge Group, Inc., "Periodic Table of Inside Sales Metrics," BridgeGroupInc.com, May 2017. See: https://blog.bridgegroupinc.com/periodic-table-inside-sales-metrics.

47 Bob Kelly, "Onboarding's Impact on Sales Productivity," SalesManagement.org, May 6, 2015. See https://salesmanagement.org/blog/onboardings-impact-on-sales-productivity.

48 Steve W. Martin, "Sales Organization Performance Gap Research Report," Stevewmartin.com, 2017. See http://wp.stevewmartin.com/sales-organization-performance-gap-research-report.

49 MRI Network, "Recruiter Sentiment Study," MRINetwork.com, December 2015. See: https://www.mrinetwork.com/media/1036/2015_recruiter_sentiment_study_2nd_half.pdf.

50   The Bridge Group, Inc., "Inside Sales for SaaS Report," HubSpot.com, 2015. See: http://cdn2.hubspot.net/hub/991/file-2448662216-pdf/2015_Inside_Sales_SaaS_report.pdf.

51   Annamarie Mann and Becky McCarville, "What Job-Hopping Employees Are Looking For," Gallup.com, November 13, 2015. See: http://www.gallup.com/businessjournal/186602/job-hopping-employees-looking.aspx.

52   United States Department of Labor, Bureau of Labor Statistics, "Number of Jobs Held, Labor Market Activity, and Earnings Growth Among the Youngest Baby Boomers: Results from a Longitudinal Survey Summary," BLS.org, March 2015. See: https://www.bls.gov/news.release/nlsoy.nr0.htm.

SECTION II: STRATEGY

53   Salesforce, "Second Annual State of Sales Report," 2017. See https://a.sfdcstatic.com/content/dam/www/ocms/assets/pdf/misc/state-of-sales-report-salesforce.pdf.

54   Aberdeen, "Sales Performance Management 2016: How The Best-In-Class Evolve Success," Aberdeen.com, 2016. See: http://v1.aberdeen.com/launch/report/research_report/11579-RR-SPM.asp.

55   Kasper Spiro, "Shocking Outcomes From ATD Research on Instructional Design," KasperSpiro.com, March 20, 2015. See https://kasperspiro.com/2015/03/20/shocking-outcomes-from-atd-research-on-instructional-design.

56   Chris Orlob, "Star Sales Reps Follow This Vital Process During Their Sales Calls," Gong.io, February 13, 2018. See https://www.gong.io/blog/sales-call-process.

57   Marc Wayshak, "The Salespeople Perceptions 2018 Survey," Marc Wayshak Sales Research & Insights, May 2018. See MarcWayshak.com/Sales-Statistics.

58   Marc Wayshak, "The Salespeople Perceptions 2018 Survey," Marc Wayshak Sales Research & Insights, May 2018. See MarcWayshak.com/Sales-Statistics.

59   Aberdeen, "Foster Marketing And Sales Alignment, Or Forget About Hitting Your Goals," Aberdeen.com, 2017. See: http://v1.aberdeen.com/launch/report/research_report/16091-RR-Marketing-Sales-Alignment-AM.asp.

60   James B. Oldroyd, Kristina McElheran and David Elkington, "The Short Life Of Online Sales Leads," HBR.org, March 2011. See: https://hbr.org/2011/03/the-short-life-of-online-sales-leads.

61   Dave Gerhardt, "We Tested The Response Time Of 433 Sales Teams. Here Are The Results," Drift.com, February 27, 2017. See: https://blog.drift.com/lead-response-survey.

62   HubSpot, "State of Inbound Report 2017," StateofInbound.com, 2017. See: http://www.stateofinbound.com.

63   HubSpot, "State of Inbound Report 2015," HubSpot.com, 2015. See https://research.hubspot.com/the-state-of-inbound-2015.

64   Marc Wayshak, "The Salespeople Perceptions 2018 Survey," Marc Wayshak Sales Research & Insights, May 2018. See MarcWayshak.com/Sales-Statistics.

65   Thomas International, "North American Sales Study," ThomasInternational.net, 2017. See: https://www.thomasinternational.net/getmedia/24319499-d393-46e0-bba8-3bad8e95a794/Thomas-Sales-Study_V1.pdf.

66   Marc Wayshak, "The Salespeople Perceptions 2018 Survey," Marc Wayshak Sales Research & Insights, May 2018. See MarcWayshak.com/Sales-Statistics.

67   Mimi An, "Buyers Speak Out: How Sales Needs to Evolve," HubSpot.com, April 7, 2016. See https://research.hubspot.com/buyers-speak-out-how-sales-needs-to-evolve.

68   Bryan Gonzales, "Sales Development Technology: The Stack Emerges," TOPOhq.com, 2017. See http://blog.topohq.com/sales-development-technology-the-stack-emerges.

69   David Mayer and Herbert M. Greenberg, "What Makes a Good Salesman," HBR.org, 2006. See https://hbr.org/2006/07/what-makes-a-good-salesman.

70   Steve W. Martin, "B2B Buyer Persona Research," Stevewmartin.com, 2017. See http://wp.stevewmartin.com/how-buyers-select-vendors-and-salespeople.

71   Salesforce, "State of the Connected Customer," Salesforce.com, 2016. See https://secure2.sfdcstatic.com/assets/pdf/misc/socc-2016.pdf.

72   DemandBase, "The 2016 B2B Buyers Survey Report," DemandGenReport.com, 2016. See https://www.demandgenreport.com/resources/research/2016-b2b-buyer-s-survey-report.

73   Chris Orlob, "The Science of Winning Sales Conversations," Gong.io, April 10, 2017. See: https://www.gong.io/blog/winning-sales-conversations.

74   Gong.io, "Tips for Optimizing Your Sales Process Using Gong.io and Sisense." See: https://player.vimeo.com/video/266426729.

75   Mark Lindwall, "Why Don't Buyers Want to Meet with Your Salespeople," Mark Lindwall's Blog, Forrester Research, September 19, 2014. See blogs.forrester.com/mark_lindwall/14-09-29-why_dont_buyers_want_to_meet_with_your_salespeople.

76   Mark Lindwall, "Why Don't Buyers Want to Meet with Your Salespeople," Mark Lindwall's Blog, Forrester Research, September 19, 2014. See blogs.forrester.com/mark_lindwall/14-09-29-why_dont_buyers_want_to_meet_with_your_salespeople.

77   David Mayer and Herbert M. Greenberg, "What Makes a Good Salesman," HBR.org, 2006. See https://hbr.org/2006/07/what-makes-a-good-salesman.

78   Paul Silvia, "Deflecting Reactance: The Role of Similarity in Increasing Compliance and Reducing Resistance," Basic and Applied Social Psychology: 27, 277-284. 2005. See: https://libres.uncg.edu/ir/uncg/f/P_Silvia_Deflecting_2005.pdf.

79   Marc Wayshak, "The Salespeople Perceptions 2018 Survey," Marc Wayshak Sales Research & Insights, May 2018. See MarcWayshak.com/Sales-Statistics.

80   Salesforce, "Second Annual State of Sales Report," 2016. See https://a.sfdcstatic.com/content/dam/www/ocms/assets/pdf/misc/state-of-sales-report-salesforce.pdf.

81   Mimi An, "Buyers Speak Out: How Sales Needs to Evolve," HubSpot.com, April 7, 2016. See https://research.hubspot.com/buyers-speak-out-how-sales-needs-to-evolve.

82   David Mayer and Herbert M. Greenberg, "What Makes a Good Salesman," HBR.org, 2006. See https://hbr.org/2006/07/what-makes-a-good-salesman.

83   Marc Wayshak, "The Salespeople Perceptions 2018 Survey," Marc Wayshak Sales Research & Insights, May 2018. See MarcWayshak.com/Sales-Statistics.

84   Gong.io, "Nine Secret Elements of Highly Effective Sales Conversations E-Book," Gong.io, February 5, 2017

85   Salesforce, "Second Annual State of Sales Report," 2017. See https://a.sfdcstatic.com/content/dam/www/ocms/assets/pdf/misc/state-of-sales-report-salesforce.pdf.

86   Chris Orlob, "These Are The Worst 13 Words To Use During Sales Calls," Gong.io.com, August 29, 2017. See https://www.gong.io/blog/worst-words-to-use-on-sales-calls.

87   Steve W. Martin, "What's Wrong with Salespeople Today," Stevewmartin.com, 2017. See http://wp.stevewmartin.com/buyers-report-whats-wrong-with-salespeople.

88   Gong.io, "Nine Secret Elements of Highly Effective Sales Conversations E-Book," Gong.io, February 5, 2017.

89   Jason Pontin, "The Importance of Feelings," MIT Technology Review, technologyreview.com, June 17, 2014. See https://www.technologyreview.com/s/528151/the-importance-of-feelings.

90   Micha Breakstone, "Deals at Risk: Chorus.Ai's Early Warning System Helps You Gain Confidence in Your Pipelines," community.choris.ai, September 28, 2017. See http://community.chorus.ai/pitch-perfect-blog/deals-at-risk-chorus-ai-s-early-warning-system-helps-you-gain-confidence-in-your-pipeline.

91   Marc Wayshak, "The Salespeople Perceptions 2018 Survey," Marc Wayshak Sales Research & Insights, May 2018. See MarcWayshak.com/Sales-Statistics.

92   Kelsey Snyder and Pashmeena Hilal, "The Changing Face of B2B Marketing," thinkwith-Google.com, Marhc 2015. See https://www.thinkwithgoogle.com/consumer-insights/the-changing-face-b2b-marketing.

93   CEB Global, "Leading B2B Sales Organizations Challenge, Align & Prescribe To Get Deals Done," news.cebglobal.com, November 21, 2016. See https://news.cebglobal.com/2016-11-21-Leading-B2B-Sales-Organizations-Challenge-Align-Prescribe-To-Get-Deals-Done.

94   Tom Atkinson and Ron Koprowski, "Sales Reps' Biggest Mistakes," HBR.org, 2006. See https://hbr.org/2006/07/sales-reps-biggest-mistakes.

95   Gong.io, "Nine Secret Elements of Highly Effective Sales Conversations E-Book," Gong.io, February 5, 2017.

96   Daniel Mochon, "Single-Option Aversion," Journal of Consumer Research, 40, October 2013; "Research Watch," Harvard Business Review, 30, October 2013.

97   Ned Welch, "A Marketer's Guide to Behavioral Economics," McKinsey Quarterly, February 2010, 4.

98   Nicholas Toman, Brent Adamson and Cristina Gomez, "The New B2B Sales Imperative," HBR.org, 2017. See https://hbr.org/2017/03/the-new-sales-imperative.

99   Rachel Young, "Buyer-Centric Sales Presentations That Win," Rachel Young's Blog, SiriusDecisions, December 29, 2015. See www.siriusdecisions.com/Blog/2015/December/BuyerCentric-Sales-Presentations-That-Win.aspx.

100 Mimi An, "Buyers Speak Out: How Sales Needs to Evolve," HubSpot.com, April 7, 2016. See https://research.hubspot.com/buyers-speak-out-how-sales-needs-to-evolve.

101 M. Reed, J. Lange, J. Ketchie, and J. Clapp, "The Relationship Between Social Identity, Normative Information, and College Student Drinking," Social Influence 2 (2007): 269–94. See: http://www.tandfonline.com/doi/abs/10.1080/15534510701476617

102 Chris Orlob, "9 Elements of Deal-Closing Sales Demos, According to New Data," Gong.io, September 14, 2017. See https://www.gong.io/blog/sales-demos.

103 Kevin L. Blankenship and Traci Y. Craig, "Language and persuasion: Tag questions as powerless speech or as interpreted in context," Journal of Experimental Psychology 43, 2007: 112-118.

104 Dr. Thomas Steenburgh, Module Note: Personal Selling and Sales Management (Boston: Harvard Business School Press, 2006) 4.

105 Gong.io, "Nine Secret Elements of Highly Effective Sales Conversations E-Book," Gong.io, February 5, 2017.

106 Matthew Dixon and Brent Adamson, The Challenger Sale: Taking Control of the Customer Conversation (Portfolio/Penguin: 2011).

107 CSO Insights, "Running Up the Down Escalator: 2017 CSO Insights World-Class Sales Practices Report," CSOinsights.com, 2017. See https://www.csoinsights.com/wp-content/uploads/sites/5/2017/08/2017-World-Class-Sales-Practices-Report.pdf

108 Salesforce, "Second Annual State of Sales Report," 2017. See https://a.sfdcstatic.com/content/dam/www/ocms/assets/pdf/misc/state-of-sales-report-salesforce.pdf.

Section III: Infrastructure

109 Dave Stein, The Top 7 Sales Training Pitfalls & 7 Solutions for Sustained Success (ES Research Group: 2012).

110 Heather Baldwin, "The (Strange) Case of the Vanishing Sales VP," SellingPower.com, July 21, 2010. See https://www.sellingpower.com/2010/07/21/9183/the-strange-case-of-the-vanishing-sales-vp.

111 Daniel McGinn, "Getting Beyond 'Show Me the Money': An Interview with Andris Zoltners," HBR.org, April 2015. See https://hbr.org/2015/04/getting-beyond-show-me-the-money-2.

112 Glassdoor Team, "How to Recruit Sales Professionals," Glassdoor.com, June 19, 2014. See: https://www.Glassdoor.com/employers/blog/recruit-sales-profes-sionals-68-job-hunting-year-Glassdoor-survey.

113 Marc Wayshak, "The Salespeople Perceptions 2018 Survey," Marc Wayshak Sales Research & Insights, May 2018. See MarcWayshak.com/Sales-Statistics.

114 Steve W. Martin, "Sales Compensation Research," Stevewmartin.com, 2017. See http://wp.stevewmar-tin.com/sales-compensation-research.

115 The Bridge Group, Inc., "Inside Sales for SaaS Report," HubSpot.com, 2015. See: http://cdn2.hubspot.net/hub/991/file-2448662216-pdf/2015_Inside_Sales_SaaS_report.pdf.

116 TinyPulse, "Employee Engagement Report: The Broken Bridges of the Workplace," TinyPulse.com, 2017. See https://www.tinypulse.com/2017-employee-engagement-report-workplace-trends-culture-transparency-performance-reviews.

117 Mimi An, "How Salespeople Learn," HubSpot.com, June 12, 2017. See https://research.hubspot.com/how-salespeople-learn.

118 Chris Orlob, "This Is How A Bad Quarter Starts In Sales," SalesHacker.com, August 15, 2017. See https://www.saleshacker.com/bad-sales-quarter.

119 Salesforce, "Second Annual State of Sales Report," 2017. See https://a.sfdcstatic.com/content/dam/www/ocms/assets/pdf/misc/state-of-sales-report-salesforce.pdf.

120 HubSpot, "State of Inbound Report 2017," HubSpot.com, 2017. See http://www.stateofinbound.com.

121 Salesforce, "Second Annual State of Sales Report," 2017. See https://a.sfdcstatic.com/content/dam/www/ocms/assets/pdf/misc/state-of-sales-report-salesforce.pdf.

122 Frank V. Cespedes and Bob Marsh, "Find the Right Metrics for Your Sales Team," HBR.org, August 2017. See https://hbr.org/2017/08/find-the-right-metrics-for-your-sales-team.

123 InsideSales.com, "Time-Based Closing Strategies: The High Cost of Procrastination," February 2017. See https://www.insidesales.com/research-paper/time-based-closing-strategies.

124   Marc Wayshak, "The Salespeople Perceptions 2018 Survey," Marc Wayshak Sales Research & Insights, May 2018. See MarcWayshak.com/Sales-Statistics.

125   Marc Wayshak, "The Salespeople Perceptions 2018 Survey," Marc Wayshak Sales Research & Insights, May 2018. See MarcWayshak.com/Sales-Statistics.

126   Roz Bahrami, "Is Bite-Size Learning the Way to Engage the Modern Distracted Learner?" TrainingIndustry.com, March 23, 2015. See https://www.trainingindus-try.com/articles/learning-technologies/is-bite-size-learning-the-way-to-engage-the-modern-distracted-learner.

127   CSO Insights, "2016 CSO Insights Sales Enablement Optimization Study," CSOInsights.com, 2017. See https://www.csoinsights.com/wp-content/uploads/sites/5/2016/08/2016-Sales-Enablement-Optimiza-tion-Study.pdf.

128   Lynette Ryals and Iain Davies, "Do You Really Know Who Your Best Salespeople Are?" Harvard Business Review, HBR.org, December 2010. See: https://hbr.org/2010/12/vision-statement-do-you-really-know-who-your-best-salespeople-are.

129   SiriusDecisions, "State of Sales Onboarding Report," HighSpot.com, 2017. See https://p.highspot.com/SD-State-of-OB-17.html.